LILLIAN TOO'S 168
Feng Shui Ways
to Declutter
Your Home

Sterling Publishing Co., Inc.
New York

For picture credits, see page 159. Every attempt has been made
to contact image copyright holders; we apologize for any omission,
in which case the UK publisher should be contacted.

Published by Cico Books Ltd
32 Great Sutton Street
London EC1V 0NB

Designed by Jerry Goldie

10 9 8 7 6 5 4 3 2 1

Published in 2003 by Sterling Publishing Company, Inc.
387 Park Avenue South, New York, NY 10016

Distributed in Canada by Sterling Publishing
c/o Canadian Manda Group, One Atlantic Avenue, Suite 105
Toronto, Ontario, Canada M6K 3E7

Library of Congress Cataloging-in-Publication Data Available

Printed in Singapore

ISBN 1 4027 0610 3

Dedication
This book is dedicated to Chris and Jenn - remember darlings,
a home free of clutter keeps the chi moving.
　　　　　　　　Mummy

Contents

Introduction

The Chinese have always viewed life as a cyclical manifestation of yin and yang moments. Life is seen by them in the context of good and bad times.

Good times can change to bad times in the same way that depressed phases of your life can transform into good periods when life moves smoothly and all seems well. The happy and unhappy periods you experience are reflected in the auric layers that cocoon you. These auric layers mirror the energy behind your feelings and emotions. They also echo the individual quality of your spirit as well as the energy of the environment surrounding you.

Thus, yin and yang forces move in the cosmic air around you. How they influence your well-being reflects the trinity of luck– i.e., heaven, earth, and mankind luck–that affects all human beings.

There are, however, aspects of your life you cannot control. These concern what is termed "heaven luck" – i.e., the destiny that is yours the moment you are born into the world. Heaven luck accounts for a third of the energies that influence your well-being.

There are also "earth luck" and "mankind luck"–which are both within your control and which, together, can be powerful enough to overcome any negative luck decreed by your heaven luck. Earth luck is the quality of energy of your living space, and mankind luck manifests the quality of the individual self.

The good news is that when your auric layers become tired or the vigor of your space stagnates, you can revitalize and re-energize the energy that affects your life.

Developing energy-awareness

When you tune into the chi that envelops you, you begin to become more aware of energy. This awareness is very powerful, as it helps you develop an eye and a feeling for the cosmic energies that affect your well-being. It also empowers the re-energizing of stagnant chi and unblocks obstacles that impede the movement of chi.

This always brings good luck, since it entices back the positive glow that accompanies a strong flow of energy within you, renewing your confidence. Such changes create powerful healing where there may have been illness, build harmony where there may have been discord, and reintroduce a fabulous new-found strength where there has been weakness.

Then you will find that bad luck stops and good luck flows unimpeded back into your life. When you shrug off old baggage and clear the clutter of your space, you will feel lighter. As you cleanse your auric fields of afflictions and negative things, and clear your spaces of stale energy, you will feel mentally clearer. You will feel more confident as you re-activate the vibrant yang chi of your body and the space you live in. As your good feelings expand, so also will your good fortune markedly improve.

There are different ways to develop your awareness of energy. Basically, you must tune in to the frequency of other vibrations. Through this, you will develop sensitivity to how different energies manifest and bounce off the physical essences, or energy, in the space surrounding you. You can sense when this essence is pure and powerful, and when it is polluted and weak. You can sense when it is whole and functioning at optimum levels, and when it is broken or injured. Energy is an intangible, invisible presence that is, nonetheless, powerfully potent.

When you dial into your own personal auric field, you will feel the hidden sensations that throb and pulsate around your physical body. These are layers of energy that create an all-encompassing halo around it. If you tune into your aura, you become more sensitive to external stimuli, and understand more keenly how your energy field affects you.

You can also develop a feeling for the air and energy that pervade your living and working spaces. The method to use is simple. All you need do is to make a conscious effort to sense the energy in the air that you breathe. Sometimes it helps if you close your eyes lightly, as this makes it easier to bring your attention to all the things in your living space. Consciously call on all of your five senses so that, in addition to your sense of sight, you also consciously engage your senses of smell, hearing, touching and tasting. It is then that you will realize just how easy it is to be oblivious to the multitude of things around you.

Living in the moment

When you are truly living in the moment–a state of "conscious knowing"–you will notice all the junk you have accumulated over the years: the magazines and newspapers that have piled up in corners, the layers of gathered dust that has gathered on furniture surfaces, and under chairs and tables. In short, you will become aware of the clutter in cupboards and cabinets, the stale food in the refrigerator, the corpses of dead insects in ceiling corners, and the grime that builds up on walls, floors, and ceilings.

And when you tune inwards into your spontaneous reactions and attitudes, you can also become acutely conscious of your negative thoughts, your prejudices, the tired way you view the relationships in your life, the soggy way you respond to the business of living. You realize then that you have allowed yourself to degenerate into a terrible state of boredom, depression, and exhaustion.

Yin energy has taken control and is dominating our lives. We stagnate, and unless we do something our lives will soon reflect the sterility and staleness of decline.

So how does junk pile up? How does dirt build up? How do lives become cluttered and clogged with bad energy? How do you get stuck in a rut, allowing your mind and attitudes to grow tired and lethargic?

Physical and spiritual dejunking

Unless you make a conscious effort to regularly clear your life of the physical and mental junk that builds up over time, there will eventually come a moment when your energy sphere will become so weakened and stale that the yin factor will penetrate your auric layers and really damage your life.

At this point, illness may set in. Physically, mentally, and even spiritually, you may feel sapped, and you weaken physically and succumb to disease. It is vital to keep all the energies that surround you vibrant and alive, which creates new pathways for the soul to grow, develop, and florish.

Techniques of cleansing, purifying, and revitalizing negative energy are found among many of the traditions of the world. The methods I use to lighten and brighten the energy around me come from my Chinese background and so they tend to be Taoist in origin, but I have also learned some truly impressive ways to purify what is spiritually negative through my studies of Buddhist esoterica. My research into purifying my auric field and space has led me to practices from other spiritual traditions, and these have added new dimensions to and enriched my practice of revitalizing energy.

I am thrilled to be able to write this wonderful book and share these very precious techniques–some of them very secret indeed–that have been given to me in wondrous and most unexpected circumstances. I have tried all of the 168 ways of revitalizing energy selected for inclusion in this book, and have had wonderful experiences with them.

The different techniques described here signify more than the mere clearing out of old and unwanted baggage. I also have included procedures for transforming energy, strengthening energy fields, and empowering energy objects. The methods recommended vary from simple step-by-step energy cleansing suggestions to rather more challenging visualizations. The use of physical implements or tools such as crystals, salt, rice grains, herbs, incense, flower petals, fragrant water, and so forth, are also included here.

Opening channels, unblocking energy

Revitalizing your life and your home should be an exciting, joyous activity. This is because this kind of work opens up channels and unblocks the energy flow so that light and chi may permeate every pore of your body and every atom of space around you. Revitalizing energy always causes some kind of transcendence to occur. You transcend into higher levels of consciousness, and sometimes into altered states of awareness and coexisting realms of reality. These different realms are in harmony when their energies are able to flow unimpeded. When there is harmony, all the feelings and emotions that pervade any living space and any living person are also in harmony. Revitalizing energy in your home involves appeasing

strident forces that could have come into it from other people or antique furniture, or that may be lingering there, left over from another time, stuck to walls, floors, and ceilings. Strident energy can also come from the recent past history of a home's inhabitants, or even from your very own past lifetimes. It is good to remember that your aura and home are affected not only by the physical objects, shapes, and forms that surround you, but also by ghost-like, lingering energy permeating time and space.

Another energy emanates from other forms of living beings, so that a different kind of spiritual energy field also exists alongside you. Trees and plants, and even the air you breathe, exude energy. The earth emits energy; insects and birds transmit energy. Also, there are spirits from other realms who may be felt as concentrations of energy. All of these add to, or subtract from, the total energy of your living space.

So all of life is energy, and everything affects you. There is a physical/spiritual interconnection of energy between you and your home. Spiritual afflictions in this energy field cause breakdowns in the physical realm, and vice versa. Any exercise in revitalizing your surrounding energy must embrace an awareness of this range of phenomena. When you accept all this, it becomes easy to move chi, easy to shift the energy within you, your home, and, thus, your life. In doing so, you transform and revitalize it. All pulsating energies surrounding and within you tend to merge so that you take on the energy of your home, and your home takes on the essence of you.

I   Tuning into the life force–the chi

Everyone can develop greater sensitivity to energy, the divinely charged spirit that gives life to us and to our homes. It is an intangible life force that molds our emotions, defines our moods, sustains our strength, and feeds our being. At birth, this spirit is pure and fresh, but as one grows into maturity and old age, it becomes colored by our experiences of life. Some of these colors expand our horizons; others make us wilt.

When we move into a brand-new home with its clean, pure energy, the smell of paint still lingering in its rooms, the spirit of the home seems vital and vibrant. When a home's life force is lively and dominated by vibrant yang energy, its inhabitants' moods tend to be positive and happy.

Over time, the energy of the home grows stale and tired. Exhaustion creeps in when yin chi accumulates, overwhelming the vitality of yang chi. Unless the energy of the home is revitalized, the chi becomes stale, bringing weakness and lethargy to its inhabitants. Their vitality suffers; good luck gets caught in a negative spiral so that, at best, boredom becomes the order of the day and, at worst, serious misfortunes, illnesses, and accidents occur. Happiness becomes an increasingly rare thing in such households.

A Kirlian image of hands that expresses the body's auric energy as an imprint.

Every living thing is thought to emit a life force, or chi. This can be captured by aura photography, which reveals intrinsic energy as color.

What causes tired energy?
Mainly it is clutter–physical, emotional, and spiritual clutter–that engulfs spaces and faces. It preys on us like an invisible monster, silently creeping into our homes and draining the energy there, When we finally become aware of its presence, our energies are already so sapped that we often lack the motivation to get rid of it.

The most debilitating effect of clutter is the way it convolutes energy within space. Although not all clutter that builds up is bad, much of it is.

Everyone needs to do chi maintenance–of the home, mind, and body. We need to clean out the stale energy created by the junk that builds up in our homes, mental attitudes, and hearts. This dejunking process will revitalize us as nothing else can. When you do this, you brush away bad energy, shrugging off outdated attitudes and making space for new energy to enter.

Chi is the cosmic breath of the universe   2

The cosmic breath, or chi energy, breathes life into all things. In recent years, the world has begun to recognize the existence of this powerfully potent life force, so that people are beginning to look at spatial and human energy in fresh new ways. Today almost everyone has heard of the cosmic breath, and many have attempted to tune into it. Ancient traditions refer to the harnessing of this cosmic life energy, and under the umbrella of feng shui practice, the balancing, clearing, and harmonizing of homes' spatial and time chi has become a popular practice.

Chi energy for life

Other practices also refer to the need to ensure the movement of chi. These include physical exercises like chi kung and tai chi, and Chinese traditional medicine and acupuncture. All enhance health and cleverly help to maintain personal chi so that the meridians of the body, along which chi moves, never become blocked. Feng shui uses the same principles to influence the chi of habitations. The smooth flow of vibrant yang chi in your home is vital to your well-being.

Tuning in to chi is not a profound exercise. Chi is something that everyone has lived with since birth; to tune in to it, all that is required is to consciously focus your attention on the invisible energy that is within and around you.

Over time, it is possible to feel the flow and movement of chi, and also to discern differences in the quality of chi in different places, and around people. Every person radiates a different kind of chi; this is reflected in the intensity of colors in a person's aura. Inanimate objects also emanate energy; however, its qualities differ according to their placement, shape, size, color, and provenance.

Energy can be friendly or hostile, nurturing or harming; embracing or strangling, clean or dirty, yin or yang. The quality of energy influences your happiness and fortune. To enjoy good fortune, you need vibrant yang chi, which supports the life of your body and your home.

Furniture with rounded edges creates a smooth path of chi (see right) which creates a positive atmosphere.

3 Becoming aware of inner vibrations

Taoist Sages who have developed mastery over their physical bodies speak frequently of the life force, which they describe as spiritual breath. Think of chi as this breath.

Before trying to tune into the chi of the space surrounding you, practice the simple chi kung exercise here to awaken the chi within you. It is also excellent for revitalizing you in the mornings. When you breathe, consciously focus your mind on the "in" and the "out" breath. Then observe your breathing for a few moments. You will soon know if it is deep or shallow, easy or requires effort. Shortness of breath is often the first sign of a hidden ailment or blockage.

Breathing also creates vibrations within your body. Vibrations that are rhythmic and regular indicate good health. Breathing that is blocked or afflicted may indicate hidden problems in your body.

An ambience of good feeling occurs when your personal vibrations beat in harmony with the vibrations radiating from the space surrounding you. Good energy interchange makes relationships run smoothly, plans move ahead, and good fortune and good feelings prevail.

Tuning in with Chi Kung

1. Relax your arms and your hands by gently shaking them. Stand erect and alert but relaxed, and position your feet as far apart as the width of your shoulders. Place both of your hands loosely by your sides, with your palms open and facing backward as shown.

2. Gently lift your arms upwards until vertical above your head, bringing the palms (still open) to face the front. As you lift your arms, stretch them high and breathe in through your nostrils. Focus your attention on your palms.

3. Next, gently lower your hands about six inches, so that your palms are now facing downwards at about 45 degrees. As you do this, breathe out through your mouth. Breathe out slowly, blowing out the air gently. Hold this position for a few moments.

4. Still holding this position, stand on tiptoe and try to remain balanced. The idea is to stretch as high as you can, while continuing to breathe.

Do this exercise at least seven times and you will feel a kind of force on your palms. Sometimes it tingles; other times, it has a heavy sensation. This is your chi.

The energy of your physical space   4

In many instances, disharmony is due to afflictions in surrounding space. These can be due to any number of physical and intangible afflictions–wrong feng shui, harmful orientations, poison arrows, killing energy, or simply stale, tired energy that has become too yin.

This last category can be the most harmful of all. It may be caused by nothing more than a daily buildup of stale, tired energy. When homes are not properly maintained, over time their energy deteriorates.

Yin chi is created by dead insects, peeling paint, damp newspapers and magazines, dying plants, and junk built up over time. When stuff has been piled in corners, hidden in closets, swept under carpets, and pushed behind curtains, while objects have not been moved for a long time, the stillness itself causes yin chi to build up. And when homes become dirty, over time grime also builds up. This kind of energy decline can be dangerous.

Gifts retained for sentimental reasons and unwanted objects left lying around create negative energy pockets all over the home which can overtake good energy sources. The energy of a home's physical space then becomes afflicted so that it has to be cleared, cleansed, and purified.

Chi and physical health

The good news is that dejunking your home is easy and revitalizing, making you feel well in the process. Clearing clutter and energizing your living and working spaces is both therapeutic and beneficial. I have found this makes such a difference to my family's sense of well-being that I have become addicted to it. My daughter says I am a compulsive dejunker. While others do spring cleaning once a year, I do it regularly, all the time.

This is because I live in a house that has grown progressively larger over the years. Space for my husband's, my daughter's, and my own rubbish to accumulate has also grown, and, unless I constantly counter our tendency to accumulate junk, the energy of my home is certain to become blocked.

However, house-clearing and rearranging my furniture and decorative objects is never a chore for me. I love keeping the chi of my house flowing smoothly – it creates a feel-good ambience in the home that I have become addicted to.

Homes need constant reorganization and effective storage to avoid the buildup of clutter and promote a balanced, harmonious environment.

5   Sensing energy from other dimensions

Before we get into the practical task of dejunking, it is useful to acknowledge that our homes are also occupied by beings from other realms of existence. These emanate energy that may cross over to our physical realm of existence–so it is possible that ghosts and other migratory beings could make their presence felt in the places where we live. Not all of us have the special "eye" to see or feel alien energy and presence of such beings, but I want to reassure those of you who do that there is nothing hostile about them. Such beings generally do not do harm unless provoked. You need not fear them, but you must have a healthy respect for them.

Sometimes, a home that has been unoccupied can feel eerie; this is the surest indication compelling yin energy is hidden somewhere within it. Ghosts emanate this type of chi and that is why graveyards are such yin places, capable of making your hair rise and your skin crawl.

Lighting transforms yin energy to yang, and can be effective in older properties that may have more residual yin energy from previous occupants. If you don't have the benefit of natural light, use spotlights and daylight (UV) bulbs to simulate vital yang chi.

How yang cures deadly yin energy

The best way to deal with such energy is to counter it with massive doses of yang energy, such as loud sounds, bright lights, and large quantities of fresh air and sunlight. Thus, the mere act of opening windows and doors to let the sunshine in will instantly make you feel better. It is not unlike cutting through thick undergrowth to bring sunlight to yin-drenched plants.

Taking a mineral salt bath banishes lingering yin chi. You can also use salt and salt water solutions to cleanse crystals (see Tips 80, 104).

If you experience a strange presence when visiting someone or some old building, make sure none of the yin chi sticks to your body or clothes. Shake your hands vigorously and visualize all yin chi being flung off you as you leave. Back home, take a salt bath, dissolving either rock salt or sea salt into the bath water, and you will have cleared off any lingering yin chi. It really is that simple.

It is possible that homes can be "invaded" by a yin presence from a different realm – this can occur due to a variety of reasons. There are special methods for handling this sort of situation and a few are explained later when we deal with space cleansing by using symbols, mantra chanting, bowls, bells, the five elements, incense, and salt (see Chapter 3 and 4).

Breathing in morning energy 6

One of the most powerfully cleansing rituals is to breathe in fresh morning chi. Breathing in morning energy is an excellent preparation for all that you may do later in the day to clear and clean your home.

To breathe in morning energy, stand outdoors where you can see the sky and feel the air. If you live in an apartment, stand by an open window or on the balcony, if you have one. To extract the chi from the rising sun, it is better to be outdoors. Thus, if you have a garden, go outside for your morning bath of fresh new energy. Look for the east side of the garden, or stand in a quiet part of the garden facing east.

If you practice yoga, you will be familiar with the sun salutation. This is a suitable exercise to enhance your store of morning chi. Alternatively, try this chi kung exercise, which is quite similar.

Do this exercise seven times and feel the morning chi cocooning you in a soft yellow light. The best time to practice is during the early dragon hour, between 7 and 9 am. This hour is suitable for everyone, although you may also select another time that is suitable for you personally according to your Chinese Zodiac animal sign (see Tip 7).

Remember that when you sweep away dust and wash away grime, you are clearing out negative yin energy. So it is an excellent idea to strengthen your personal chi each morning with a bath of pure yang energy as a countermeasure.

Boosting Your Chi

1. Relax your body and stand with your feet a shoulder-width apart as shown.

2. Clasp your hands together tightly, but with both of your index fingers pointing upward.

3. With fingers clasped this way, stretch both hands upward, over and above your head. As you swing your hands up, breathe in through your nose.

4. Feel your chest opening as it fills with air. You are facing the East, so feel the morning sunlight bathing you with a soft glow.

5. Bend forward, allowing your clasped hands to fall between your legs. Breathe out through your mouth. Relax into the stretch.

7   A sunshine bath for yang energy

When you take a sunshine bath to replenish your yang essence, do choose a day when the weather is clear and bright. If the day is dreary, drizzling with rain, or it is snowing or about to rain, it is not a good time to replenish your chi. Although the best time for practicing this ritual is the time of the dragon, when you can tap into sunrise energy between 7 and 9 am, you can also select the hours of the Snake (9 to 11 am) to absorb early sunshine. Those who want greater intensity of sunlight can take a sunshine bath during the hours of the Horse (11 to 1 pm) or even the hours of the Sheep (1 to 3 pm) when the afternoon sun is in the sky and the sunlight is stronger and more intense. Generally, it is a good idea to choose the time that harmonizes with your own Chinese Zodiac sign.

nature often use this time when they soak in the sunshine to keep their eyes open to the things they see. For instance, if you see birds soaring, playing, or singing, it is an excellent indication that some new opportunity or good news is winging its way to you. This would also be a good day on which to practice clutter clearing and purification rituals to improve the energy of your home. On many mornings I have observed yellow-tailed birds building nests in my garden, and those days always brought wonderful new developments my way.

You too can develop a sensitivity to signals. If you tune into them frequently enough, there will soon come a time when you will be able to notice when nature is sending you a special message.

How to take a sunbath

To take a sunshine bath, stand for about three minutes in your garden or on your balcony, simply soaking up the sunlight. Those taking in stronger sunshine during the later hours should not stand in direct sunlight, but instead look for a corner of the garden or balcony where there is diffused or shaded light. Keep your facial expressions relaxed, but be alert to your surroundings. This is an excellent time to tune in to signals from nature (see Tips 8 and 9).

Taoist masters trained in reading the signals of

Zodiac Animals and Time

Those born in Dragon, Monkey, and Rat years will benefit from taking in the sunrise during the Dragon hour of 7 to 9 am.

Those born in Snake, Rooster, or Ox years will benefit from taking a sunshine bath when the sun shines a little brighter, during the Snake hour of 9 to 11 am.

Those born in Horse, Dog, and Tiger years will benefit from taking a sunshine bath when the sun has traveled higher up the horizon, during the Horse hour of 11 am to 1 pm.

Those born in Sheep, Pig, and Rabbit years will benefit from taking a sunshine bath when the sun has traveled even higher up in the sky, i.e., past noon between the hours of 1 and 3 pm, which is the hour of the Sheep.

Signals from your garden 8

Birds are only one of the ten thousand ways that Nature communicates with us, but they seem to be a favorite vehicle. The appearance of birds is always a good signal, heralding new beginnings and keeping you safe. When a particularly colorful or musical bird drops by your garden, it indicates a significant lucky event is about to occur. In Taoist feng shui, yellow birds predict happy occasions, such as a wedding, birth, or promotion.

If you are having trouble selling your house, draw a picture of a bird flying out of your house, carrying in its beak a piece of paper with your house address written on it. Hang it on the wall next to the front door. This will bring you a buyer very soon. For good measure, you can even write down the amount you want to receive on the paper.

Flowers, leaves, and fruit

Looking to nature for signals is best done when you are taking a sunshine bath during the morning hours. If you spy a significant single flower blooming, a project is coming to fruition. The blossoming of red flowers indicates love, and yellow flowers wealth. White flowers suggest a new and important friendship.

Leaves falling from trees means it's time for a major dejunk. They indicate that there is much to throw away in order to make way for new growth. The same applies if you spot an otherwise healthy plant whose leaves have turned yellow. So

Birds for protection while traveling

Hanging a yellow bird image on the rear bumper or inside the rear window of your car, protects those inside from accidents. Keeping three white bird feathers inside the glove compartment has the same effect.

Leaf or flower buds in the garden symbolize birth and beginnings.

fall is a good time to clear your home of junk, before the onset of winter.

When trees bear fruit on their left side (when looking outward from your house), it indicates a major triumph is on its way to the patriarch or husband dwelling in the house. Fruit on the tree's right side means good luck is coming to the wife. Ants coming toward the home in a convoy are always a good sign. Black ants are better than red ants. Frogs jumping into the house are extremely auspicious. A stray tortoise making its way into your garden is also a most auspicious indication. Indeed, any kind of living creature visiting you is a good sign.

9 Reading signals sent by the winds

Signs from the cosmos are also wafted to us by the winds. Usually such signals manifest the wind trigram, Sun–thus, the gentle breeze brings good tidings. When you walk into your garden or onto your apartment balcony and look towards the distant skyline, take some moments to smell the morning air and feel the breeze. Look at the clouds and the color of the sky. Taoist masters say that the presence of some pockets of clouds is always a good sign. See whether you can detect images of auspicious signs in the clouds.

When there is no breeze, it is not a good day for clearing clutter. It is the same when winds blow too strongly. When the wind seems excessively harsh, money cannot accumulate and it is a sign to get rid of dated documents, files, and papers from your office. When winds blow strongly, it is also a general warning of some kind. Invariably, if you act on messages like this from the winds, you may discover something of personal significance to you or to your loved ones that has been lost. This may take the form of information that you have forgotten about because it has been buried under that pile of papers that has been growing on your desk over the past months. So be sensitive to the signals the wind sends you.

Storms as Blessings

Signals from the wind also come in the form of quite dramatic rainstorms, complete with thunder and lightning. I recall the day my daughter got married in April of 2002. At 3.30 pm sharp, during the hour of the Monkey, a thunderstorm broke out over Kuala Lumpur that was an awesome display of the power of wind and water. Had it not abated, it would have been the perfect storm.

By five minutes to 5, however, the storm had completely disappeared. And the cloudless sky that was left behind was a heavenly blue. I read this as a marvelous sign from heaven. The rain was a shower of nectar blessings from heaven, while thunder and lightning indicated claps of approval. If the storm had started later, or had not abated, the signs would have been bad. That it cleared up and in its place had come brightness and lightness from the wind-washed sunshine was a very good sign indeed. Such signs preceding marriage or birth celebrations always come during the hour of the Monkey, between 3 and 5 pm. Subsequently, the wedding celebrations proceeded smoothly, and without a hitch.

Many instances like this have happened in my life, so I do appreciate signs from the cosmos. I also have discovered that, when using feng shui and working with energy, it is helpful to be conscious of other related esoteric aspects and phenomena, and to keep an open mind.

The pure yang chi of children 10

If you want to get an instant, accurate reading of the energy of your rooms and home, and don't want to incur the cost of engaging an expensive feng shui master, look for a young male child below the age of nine and bring him to the site you are considering. Usually the younger the child, the more accurate will be the signals he receives. What you need for this purpose is pure yang energy, and young dragon boys possess tons of this. (Girls are not considered as effective for this practice, as they are both yin and yang.)

Boys and yang energy

Boys are thought to be very sensitive to the quality of chi inside homes; bring a yang child into your home and watch him. If he cries, or becomes restless, it indicates that pockets of hostile yin energy are making him uncomfortable, and therefore the house needs cleansing.

If the child can be appeased with sweets and some cajoling, it is a good sign, since this suggests that the problem is not severe. But if he manifests negative behavior–he insists on leaving or cries, for example–it indicates something strongly negative is in the house. Negative behavior from him indicates that negative energy is present.

This short-cut method of assessing the feng shui of homes is very widely used by the Chinese. They usually bring a small baby boy with them when checking out houses or shops to rent. In Hong Kong, for example, businessmen almost always observe the behavior of young children at new premises before signing a lease on a property. If the child asks to use the bathroom, this indicates money loss and is therefore a bad omen for business.

If the child seems happy, smiles a lot, and hums to himself or, better yet, draws houses, cars and auspicious objects or brings out a toy to play with, it is a sure sign that prosperity will arise in such a place. If he takes food to eat from his pocket, it is propitious. If he brings out a building toy like building blocks, or paper for origami, it is also a good sign. If he brings out an electronic toy, it is good, but not as auspicious as if he were making something.

Just observing boys' behavior reveals a great deal about the energy-quality of a place.

When children draw happy pictures in a home, it means that the inhabitants will be prosperous.

11   The chi of time and space

The chi of the environment can be classified according to whether it is spatial chi or time chi.

What is spatial chi?
Spatial chi is created by the shape, size, and density of an object, as well as its position, in a space. Spatial chi can be studied under the auspices of the fundamental concepts of "form school" feng shui practice, which also includes the study of the symbolic meanings of decorative objects, plants, and animals. In this way, the chi of a place, and the furniture and things in that space, may be found to be good or bad, hostile or friendly, according to the spatial concepts of feng shui.

What is time chi?
Time chi is intangible and harder to visualize than spatial chi. It is based on a concept that is, by definition, invisible and without form.

If revitalizing your home involves building work, check that no negative energy will be disturbed and activated in the process.

The quality of this chi is affected by nothing more than the passage of time. It is expressed and defined in terms of compass orientations. Time chi affects a place according to the time we are studying its space.

The study of spatial energy alone is deemed to be incomplete since chi in specific parts of every home can turn hostile simply because of the date and time. When the chi of a room is hostile, you must be careful about undertaking any major spring-cleaning there. In general, rooms or corners whose chi is afflicted in a particular year should be left quiet and undisturbed during that year.

There are calculations based on the Chinese solar calendar that indicate when parts of the home must be left undisturbed. Spring-cleaning and clutter-clearing should not be undertaken in these rooms then. More importantly, rooms and sectors of the house that are afflicted in any year also should not be renovated. Banging, digging, and knocking in nails, and so forth, can cause such trauma to the chi energy that the bad luck that manifests can be quite severe.

This branch of feng shui is referred to as Flying Star. Recently, this practice has become popular due to its potency, and also the speed with which it brings results.

For our purposes, it is sufficient to learn how to observe the annual changing character of energy for defensive reasons so that we do not inadvertently disturb space and trigger misfortune.

The three taboos of time chi 12

Antidotes exist for overcoming these afflictions, based upon where they are located each year.

When not to dejunk
The main thing to note, however, are the taboos associated with their locations. Be very wary of what you simply must not do in those places that are occupied by the three afflictions, so as not to incur illness or trigger misfortunes and hardships for yourself and your family.

If the places occupied by the afflictions are disturbed by dejunking and revitalizing activities, mishaps can occur. So, if there is excessive disturbance in the place occupied by the Grand Duke, caused by excessive dejunking and cleaning, it is thought to bring failure that year. The Deadly Five Yellow brings financial loss and illness, while the Three Killings brings three kinds of bad luck associated with relationships. Because of this, it is very useful to get to know these afflictions of time chi.

Dejunking afflicted areas of the home can create misfortune rather than new opportunities.

There are three annual Flying Star afflictions, and their locations must be checked each year before making major changes to the home. This ensures that, in trying to improve the quality of chi, you do not unintentionally make things worse. It is also necessary to learn how to take countermeasures to diffuse these three afflictions, especially when they affect the chi of the bedroom or hit the main door of the home. Being aware of these annual afflictions adds the vital dimension of time to whatever you do to enhance and revitalize your living space.

Each affliction occupies different angles and directions in space. The Grand Duke Jupiter occupies only 15 degrees of the compass; the Deadly Five Yellow, 45 degrees, and the Three Killings, 90 degrees.

Degrees of Affliction

The three major afflictions in every year are:
- the Grand Duke Jupiter
- the Deadly Five Yellow
- the Three Killings.

The Five Yellow afflicts 45 degrees of the compass and the south area of a room or home in 2004, so this sector must be left alone for the twelve months of this year.

North

13 The annual Five Yellow chi

The Five Yellow is the most deadly of the three annual afflictions, especially in years when it flies into the earth and fire element sectors of the compass. This happened in 1999 when it flew to the South, a fire element sector, and in 2001 when it flew into the Southwest, an earth element sector. In these two sectors, the Five Yellow, being an earth-element affliction, is considerably strengthened, making it more dangerous. The Five Yellow simply must not be disturbed or activated. When this happens, it brings severe illness, financial loss, and obstacles to success.

Fire and the Five Yellow

The Five Yellow is at its most dangerous when it is magnified by fire energy. Therefore, rituals for revitalizing chi that use lights and incense, when done in a corner of the home occupied by the Five Yellow, can be quite dangerous. The negative chi of Five Yellow becomes magnified by this. If the space is also occupied by the main door or bedroom, its bad effect can be very severe. In 2003, the Five Yellow occupies the Southeast, in the vicinity of the wood element; therefore, this part of the house should not be disturbed or activated with fire element energy during that year. Also refrain from undertaking any renovations here, such as building new shelves or cupboards. There should be no digging, cutting, sawing of wood, or excessive noise. These safeguards must be observed each year in sectors occupied by the Five Yellow; otherwise, you will inadvertently activate its energies. Let the corner it occupies remain undisturbed. If you are desperate to clear the clutter in your home, and need to make bookshelves or move new furniture into an afflicted sector, and simply cannot delay doing this until the following year, then at least make sure you do not begin any such activity in the sector where it resides.

Candles represent Fire energy, which fuel the Five Yellow.

The Five Yellow

Here is the location of Five Yellow for the next ten years. This represents one full cycle, after which it starts again.

Year	Position of the Five Yellow in the house
2003	Southeast
2004	Center
2005	Northwest
2006	West
2007	Northeast
2008,	South
2009	North
2010	Southwest
2011	East
2012	Southeast

Fire energy includes incense, which fuels the Five Yellow affliction. Ensure that fire and the Five Yellow do not reside in the same compass sector of your home.

The Grand Duke and Three Killings chi 14

The Grand Duke Jupiter (also known as the tai tsui) is an annual affliction that affects fifteen degrees of space, which correspond to the direction the year's animal sign occupies. So, in 2002, it afflicts the South, which is the direction of the Horse. In 2003, it afflicts the direction of the Sheep, and, in 2004, the direction of the Monkey. Shown in the chart here are the directions of the Grand Duke in a twelve-year cycle.

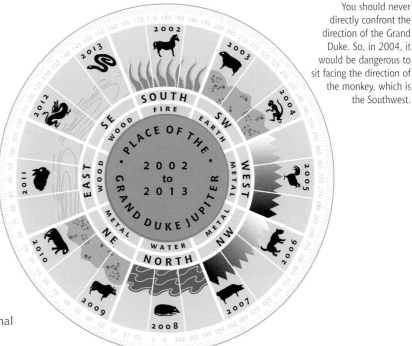

You should never directly confront the direction of the Grand Duke. So, in 2004, it would be dangerous to sit facing the direction of the monkey, which is the Southwest.

Those born in the animal year directly opposite to the ruling animal of the year are said to be in direct conflict with the Grand Duke. For example, in 2002, Rat-year people experienced conflict, as the Rat is opposite the Horse on the zodiac wheel. In Chinese astrology, those born in the animal year directly opposite the year's ruling animal tend to have a bad year. In 2003, the Grand Duke is in the Sheep direction of South/Southwest, and the Ox is opposite. Therefore, people born in the Ox year have a tough time that year. The taboos that apply to the Grand Duke direction are similar to those for the Five Yellow.

The Three Killings affliction is known as the "sarm saat" in Chinese. When you undertake repairs and renovations, it is a good idea to avoid working in the sector of the house occupied by the Three Killings. This is a troublesome taboo, since it affects a large part of the house. It covers 90 degrees of the compass; this is because the Three Killings only affects the cardinal directions of space and never the secondary directions.

Cures for the Three Killings

In the years of the Ox, Rooster, and Snake, the Three Killings affliction resides in the East. The cure for it in this area is to shine a bright light in a corner, or to hang a metal wind chime in the room it occupies.

It moves to the West in the years of the Boar, Rabbit, and Sheep. The cure for it is to shine a bright light there or to place an open container of water in the western corner.

During the years of the Monkey, Rat, and Dragon, the Three Killings affliction occupies the South. The cure for it is to set out crystals or to place an open bowl of earth there.

In Dog, Horse, and Tiger years, it resides in the North. The cure for the Three Killings there is to place plants and flowers in the North.

15 Assessing yin and yang chi

Have you ever entered someone's home and felt that the atmosphere is unbalanced, not in sync, or just seriously disturbed? If you are sensitive to energy, you might also feel sick, or as if you are choking or in need of air. Sometimes strange energy manifests in the onslaught of a massive headache. These are indications that the chi of the house or building you are visiting may be in conflict with your chi, or that perhaps the energy there is so yin that it disturbs your balance.

Yang chi sustains us. When we encounter spaces that are too yin, we react. These reactions manifest more keenly in those who have acute sensitivity to energy or in those who are accustomed to working with it.

Pay attention to yin rooms such as the bedroom and bathroom. These are quiet spaces, but they still need vitality.

Usually yin chi is experienced as sad, hostile, negative energy. If you think of all the attributes of yin, you will be able to recognize yin chi. Yin is still, quiet, immobile, cold, heavy, dark, and like death. It is not that yin chi is intrinsically bad, but in yang dwellings, which are preferred by the living, negative energy is yin and it is this manifestation of yin that is not desirable.

What is heartbreak chi?

When we focus our attention on the chi of any home, we can pick up the vibrations that dominate the house. If its occupants are sad, you will pick up a sense of pervasive melancholia. Sometimes the air can be so thick with despondency that you become imbued with despondency too. Sad homes contain illness and heartbreak chi that tends to sap the yang spirit. This is because the home is hungry for yang chi. Such homes create depression, hopelessness, and a resigned air.

It is also possible to sense killing chi, if it is present. This kind of hostility emanates from walls and ceilings. If you are sensitive to chi, you will feel the presence of invisible knives and arrows that create uncomfortable sensations. This kind of chi is very harmful and can be dangerous, causing illness, loss, and accidents to befall residents.

Houses with negative chi energy do sap their inhabitants' spiritual vitality. Such places are characterized by a strong feeling of lethargy. Homes like these really need to be revitalized and given a shot of living-movement chi.

Sensing the atmospheres of individual homes   16

Most homes contain some negative chi that has been created over time. Anger, quarrels, illness, stress, disappointments, and exhaustion all create energy that sticks to the walls, floors, and ceilings of homes. Indeed, nothing sticks to walls and floors better than loud shouting, violent quarrels, and quick tempers. These negative emotions are the stuff of heavy-laden chi that is absorbed by the living space. It is because of this that I always advocate opening doors and windows at least once a day for a few minutes to welcome in powerful yang energy of the winds, waters, and sunshine that is found in such an infinite quantity outdoors.

Homes contain a mixture of energies that have many different effects. Tuning in to the chi present will unlock some of this energy so that it moves into your consciousness. Once you know the difference between the intrinsic chi of the self and that of space, and are comfortable with the concept of spatial and time energy, that is the starting point for you to open your consciousness to all the different types of energy that exist. Then you can start to read the chi that occupies your own home. Remember that every home has its own spirit.

Many homes that contain so much love and laughter that their happiness chi just spills over from them; you can actually feel it embrace you, bathing you in a warm glow. This is what we should aim to create–a loving, warm, fresh feeling that is devoid of negativity.

The spirit of the home   17

The spirit of the home comes alive when happiness is present. This is what good feng shui is for: creating an all-pervasive feeling that makes a home's inhabitants feel strong, confident, and fulfilled.

Colors, music, children, lights, water, and sounds are such strong purveyors of yang energy that all homes should have them. They stimulate lots of yang chi which accumulates, filling the home with life.

Clever homemakers utilize these "tools" in good measure, bathing their homes with fresh color, lots of bright

Plants emanate yang energy, which creates a healthy, lively atmosphere.

light, and pleasing sounds. Curtains and tabletops are always kept clean and free of accumulations of clutter from past months and years. There may be some daily untidiness and disarray in rooms, reflecting that they are lived in, but there will not be junk, piles of unread newspapers, or any broken plates and cups left lying around.

In a healthy house, there is warmth and constantly moving energy. There is little stagnation present. This is the kind of home that has and encourages a spirit of abundance.

18   Reading energy and communicating with walls

How do I read energy? Basically, I listen. Each time people tell me about the series of aggravating events that have happened to them, I suspect that something has gone amiss in the energy of their homes so that, when I visit them, I try to communicate directly with their homes.

I always begin with five minutes of meditation, in order to calm my mind and focus on the task at hand. First, I focus on the energy of the home from its center; it is here that the vortex of the house's energy resides. Then I walk around the rooms in a clockwise direction as near to the walls as possible, lingering at the corners. My thoughts are focused on each room. My intention is to pick up strong imprints of positive and negative energies–to see where they have accumulated, and whether the rooms are still (thence, yin) or moving (therefore yang). This way, it is immediately possible to tell which parts of the home need working on the most. As I move around each room, I breathe evenly and focus my attention on the palms of my hands. Whenever I feel a force of resistance, I know that hidden somewhere nearby is bad energy.

Listening for energy

When approaching the wall nearest the door leading into the room, I place both palms on the wall and my ear against it. Then I go around the room, with my palms drawing invisible circles on the wall as I move forward. I am listening with my ear. I find that closing my eyes slightly helps me to tune in. Soon I begin to feel the tingle of chi as it transfers from the wall onto my palms. It is then that I get a feeling for how to change the flow of chi in the room and banish the aggravations that are plaguing the household.

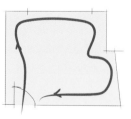

Walking clockwise around a room close to the walls helps you attune to the energy there.

Keeping energy flowing smoothly for vitality 19

Energy that is imbued with life and vitality flows smoothly – it is gentle, undulating, and relaxed. This kind of energy is completely free of tension and aggravation. It is the kind of energy we strive to create in our homes.

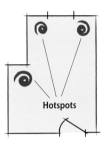

Identity the social hotspots in a room, where people tend to gather, then work on boosting the cooler, less popular corners to lift the energy overall.

Hotspots

In order to encourage this, feng shui practitioners ensure that objects are arranged around the home in a manner that enables energy to flow. The way that room layouts are planned and furniture is arranged is either conducive to or blocks energy. Energy must not remain stagnant. Blockages make energy stagnate. Energy that does not move becomes sick, while energy that moves too fast turns hostile and destructive. Energy that flows smoothly and naturally, moving neither too fast, nor too slowly, is good energy; it is friendly and brings good fortune.

Mapping successes and failures

The health of your home's energy will express itself in the events that take place in your life. Smooth-flowing energy there brings easy success to all of your plans and projects. Blocked energy creates obstacles that slow down progress, while stagnant energy brings sickness. Failure also is a direct result of blocked energy.

Learn to watch the flow of energy in your home. The easiest way to do this is to trace the way traffic moves within your house. Watch where most residents tend to gravitate. Identify rooms that simply never get used. You may think that the dining room would be used most, but if the energy there is bad, you will find your family eating out and not coming home for meals.

You can get a very good idea about the flow of energy in each room by simply observing how often it is used. Where healthy energy accumulates is where all members tend to gravitate. This is an excellent way to develop sensitivity to the energy within your own home.

As a first step, entice family members towards the center of your house. If this is also the family or dining room, it will imbue the heart of your home with vital energy. It also will bring wonderfully good energy into your home.

20 Lonely rooms

You should do something about the rooms in your home that seem to be lonely. Such rooms are usually dark and unused–and filled with stagnant energy. It is likely that there is unhappy and hostile breath within them.

Rooms that have somehow degenerated into storerooms tend to become like this. When their energy becomes too heavy, it will also permeate the floors and walls, and begin to affect the rooms above and below them. You can use temporary cures based on the five elements to correct this imbalance, but a more permanent solution is simply to get rid of any junk there–clear blockages, install bright new lights, and apply a fresh coat of paint. In other words, you should basically revitalize the chi of such rooms.

The revitalizing of chi is as much an instinctive exercise as it is an acquired expertise. Once you have learned all of the methods suggested in this book and know how to revitalize chi by using each of the five elements–fire, water, wood, metal, and earth–you will develop a familiarity with the way to do this in no time at all. Learn to listen to your home first and then use these techniques.

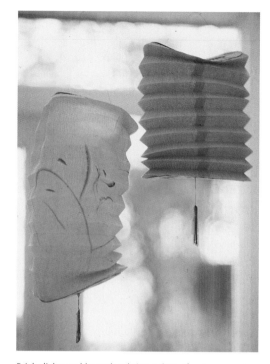

Bright lights and hot colors bring a dose of yang energy to desolate rooms.

21 Pay attention to your bedroom

Pay special attention to the rooms that are important to you and that you use most frequently. When the chi energy of your bedroom is unwelcoming, for instance, you and your spouse may feel restless and not want to come home. This is how problems in marriages begin. It is caused by the bad energy of the bedroom that the couple share. So develop sensitivity to the feelings in your bedroom.

When there is a blockage in the flow of bedroom chi, you will feel your relationship is becoming stuck. This happens when your bedroom is not cleaned enough or kept in good repair. Many young working couples allow the chi of their bedroom to deteriorate. It begins with harmless untidiness and then, before you realize it, the bedroom has become thick with unwashed clothes, bags, shoes, magazines, and sometimes even stale food. Drawers get clogged up and closets become disorganized and cramped. The bad mood of the couple also adds to this buildup, and negativity begins to dominate the room.

Your bedroom should contain friendly, embracing, chi energy. For your relationship to grow, your bedroom must have a good flow of chi, the magical life force.

My father's clutter and my mother's transformation   22

For years, my father and mother fought over the stuff he insisted on keeping. At first, it was a source of great humor between them as she laughingly nagged him to get rid of his National Geographic magazines, his trinkets and items collected over the years, and his old worn-out shirts and pajamas. But, as the years passed, she realized that she could do nothing about his incurable attachment to all of his out-dated possessions. So she lived with the clutter of their bedroom until he passed away. After his death, all that clutter became a source of severe depression for her. I saw her fall into a spiral of grief, and she became ill and desperately unbalanced. For a while, I was at a loss as to how to cope.

In desperation, I went to her home and, in a frenzy of zeal, we cleared out their bedroom. I went through everything stuffed in closets, hidden under the bed, and stacked on bookshelves. I gave his carefully bound

Too many sentimental possessions and general clutter can cause a feeling of oppression, preventing the occupants from moving forward in life.

magazines to the local library, burned his clothes, and everything else he had accumulated over the years we gave away to relatives and friends. I kept his reclining chair. Everything else we threw away. And then I bought her a new apartment on the top-most floor of a modern condominium with a huge swimming pool, a gym, a café, and lots of young people.

This forced her into a new environment that had tons of fresh yang energy. The change in her was pure joy to watch. Today she is sprightly, cheerful, and very happy. At her granddaughter's wedding early this year, she even danced the tango. At 79, she looked years younger than when she was 60!

23 Keep the flow moving–share your good possessions

The flow of energy inside your home must never be allowed to stop or become blocked. Giving away old clothes and old possessions–bags, shoes, books, accessories, trinkets, towels, even furniture–is the best way to keep the flow moving. This is because, when you give away your old things, you are, in effect, making room for new things to come into your life. Giving creates a vacuum in your storage space, and in your chests of drawers, shelves, and rooms. As soon as there is spare space available, more goodies will come into your life, in no time at all.

Remember that clearing your home of too many possessions is also clearing clutter. You don't have to clear out only useless, torn, outdated stuff. You also can get rid of possessions that are still good but that you may have outgrown. In other words, share your goodies with others. Give your good things to charities and watch your life become imbued with a shot of fresh new possessions, bringing new chi into your home.

Clutter can be beautiful if it is an item you have outgrown or no longer like. Your possessions need to reflect your present tastes and interests.

The freedom of giving

I know many very wealthy and generous people who regularly make a pile of their very beautiful possessions and donate them to a charitable cause. I am one of those fortunate people who have known and been inspired by some pretty well-heeled generous hearts. I am glad to say that these wonderful friends of mine keep growing richer and richer. And it is no surprise, either, for this creates a wonderful, natural flow of energy in their lives–and seemingly without any effort.

Needless to say, I have also seen the insides of their homes and believe me, there is little clutter. This is because they are so used to giving things away that, over time, they have developed a certain detachment towards their possessions–so junk simply has little chance to build up.

A small gift of three Chinese coins represents prosperity for the recipient.

Never block the main door   24

It is simply vital that the entrance into your home is never blocked in any way. Energy coming in must never be allowed to become stuck in any way. To begin with, your entrance doors must be able to open fully. Door hinges must be well-oiled, and the part of the wall that is behind the door must not have large pieces of furniture or anything at all that can cause the door to open only a miserable forty-five degrees.

Both inside and outside the house, the main door should enjoy the effect of a bright hall–a clear space where good chi can enter, accumulate, and settle. This flow of energy must not be blocked at or around the doorway.

The mouth of the home

The Chinese refer to the main door as the mouth of the home, the place that must enjoy auspicious features. So the ideal is to have a relatively spacious area in front of your front door. If you do not have this, and the main door foyer area is small and tight, it is all the more reason that you must make a special effort not to let the space here become cramped. The front door area of the home is no place for shelves and storage units. If the reason for the problem here is because your family has outgrown your front door space, then consider how you might create some more permanent solution.

My own home has grown larger over the years, alongside our family's rise in fortunes. When we built our home 27 years ago, we did not have much money, so we built a small house. But, over the years, as our needs have become more sophisticated, we have begun to require more space. So, instead of one living room, we now have three. In expanding our home, however, I always have made sure that the front door was left pristinely clear of furniture, cabinets, and book-shelves. There is a minimum of built-in shelves and cupboards in my living room–in fact, I have only one. This is because I do not want junk to get shut inside, thus accumulating harmful yin energy. The only side cupboard we have, and which I clear at the end of each year, always contains junk. No matter what I do or how careful I am about not filling it with junk, it somehow gets filled up. So now I consciously fill it with goodies–incense, candles, aroma oils–things we use throughout the year so that, over time, this cupboard simply clears itself.

Keep clutter to a minimum by the front door, or opportunities are symbolically blocked.

25   Correcting clashing elements at the doorway

Bad energy at the door can be the result of element clash. The five elements of feng shui are fire, wood, metal, earth, and water. The elements have a productive and destructive cycle.

Knowing about elements enables you to sense when there is discord in the energy flow of your house and how this can be transformed into harmony. Thus, when your door is sited in either of the wood corners (Southeast or East) of the house, it should not be painted white or made of metal, e.g., an aluminum sliding door. This is because metal destroys wood and is bad for the energy of that location. Wooden doors are best,

particularly painted blue, as water produces wood. But a door painted red will make your household very tired and exhausted. This is because fire energy exhausts wood energy.

When the main door location corresponds to the earth directions (Southwest or Northeast), then do not have a green door of young wood. Old wood is fine, because fast-growing wood energy is harmful for earth corners, depleting them of energy. The result of this can be very harmful, causing illness and the drying-up of opportunities. In the metal corners (Northwest and West), red doors are a danger.

26   Dissolving bad energy at the front door

There is nothing more harmful to the home than a front door that is cracked or chipped, or whose paint is peeling. If your door has a crack in it, or its hinges creak, it is really important to change or repair it. Sometimes, due to weather conditions, wooden doors expand and then they scrape the bottom of the floor. This should be attended to immediately since it portends accidents to the home's residents. It also makes the door get stuck; this, in turn, makes your life get stuck too!

Doors that are clearly flawed, with holes or cracks in them, are very dangerous for a house's inhabitants. They are signs that something is not right with the chi around

A front door painted in bright, fresh colors is good feng shui practice.

the doorway. So you should not only get the door repaired but also revitalize the chi of the doorway by brightening it with lights. Also, use incense to clear bad vibrations. Keep the place well-lit for at least a week, and treat it to a fresh coat of paint.

Bad energy at the doorway is caused by creaking hinges–which must be oiled immediately. Indeed, this is something I do at least once every six months; I go around all my doors and windows and I oil their hinges. This ensures that all doors open and close smoothly for me so that neither the danger of lost opportunities nor of imprisonment is created. The doors in my home open and close easily–yours should too.

Empowering a front door with protective energy 27

When your entrance door is strong, it possess powerful protective energy. When I visited the spiritual island of Bali this year, I noticed that special attention was always accorded to the entrance of buildings. The guide explained that having a split-totem effect at the gate signified powerful protective energy, since the doorway could close instantly and merge into a guardian totem.

The Chinese empower their entrances with protective door gods, especially in temples and palaces, and with a pair of Chi Lin or Fu dogs in homes. You will discover, as I did, that so many cultures and traditions of the world believe in the power of guardian symbols for doorways. These are usually placed at the entrances to homes. Symbols become more powerful when you consciously empower the doorway with vital energy. Empowerment comes from focused concentration and appropriate visualization.

Animal symbols on doors and gateposts are popular emblems of protection. In Western and Eastern cultures, lions and birds formally depicted in bronze and stone guard their territory.

Visualization empowerments are best done in the morning at sunrise. First, shake your hands three times to loosen the flow of energy. Stand just inside the house, about nine feet (2.75 m) away from the front door. Hold up your hands, with palms open, so your whole body faces the closed door. Focus your mind on the door and imagine an invisible energy force coming from your palms and lighting up the doorway area in the space just in front of the door. Think to yourself that this energy is an invisible wall of strong, protective light that prevents hostile energy from entering.

How to Protect Your Door

If your doorway is facing South, your door is sitting North. Visualize a sheet of blue light which keeps out bad luck and bad people.

If your door faces East, create a mental sheet of white light. This protects the home from evil entities and misfortunes.

If your door faces West, think of a sheet of green or blue light. This brings in growth energy and protects residents from misfortunes.

If your door faces North, you will be sitting South, so think of a sheet of glowing light pink–this attracts energy that is very strongly protective.

If your door is facing Southwest or Northeast, imagine a sheet of yellow light that is glowing like gold. This is a powerful visualization and is excellent for empowering your door so that it will attract the nine types of good fortune.

If your door is facing Southeast, visualize a wall of white light in order to attract good fortune from heaven luck.

And if your door is facing Northwest, think of a wall of blue or green light. This brings prosperity.

28   What saps you of energy?

When you feel tired all the time, losing inspiration, motivation, and sight of your goals in life, you may want to take a look around your living space. When the energy of your home or room is tired, you will find this tiredness transferred to you–so that you feel exhausted and depleted of energy.

This usually indicates that something inside the room, or home, is sapping it of its energy. Tiredness is the mildest result of this kind of afflicted energy. Sometimes it causes weaker inhabitants to grow sick.

Feeling tired and lethargic can be due to an energy imbalance in your home.

Being a room detective

Consciously tune in to your home and meditate to find the cause of this malaise. When you attune your mind to the same frequency as your home, you are almost certain to discover the source of the affliction, and the cause of what is wrong. Go into each room–especially the room you spend the most time in–and look for holes in the walls, broken shelves, broken equipment, broken vases and urns, or, worse yet, porcelain statues that have hairline cracks or chips. Also, dirty storerooms or unused, neglected rooms cause negative chi.

Married couples who often feel too tired for each other should investigate their bedroom–some quality of this room could be sapping them of their energy. If the bed is in poor condition (say, if the headboard or frame is damaged or the mattress has a broken spring) this symbolically says that the couple's relationship is also starting to crack. So have whatever is broken or chipped replaced–it is worth the expense. Not doing so could lead to the relationship deteriorating.

Broken Pots Bring Bad Luck

The Chinese are very superstitious about having something broken inside the house, especially if it is a porcelain vase, a ceramic urn, or some earth-based container. It is believed that these broken containers sap space of its vital energy. Broken bathtubs, sinks, and toilets are equally bad. Unless these broken items are removed or replaced, the luck of a home turns negative.

Throw out chipped and broken utensils 29

Chinese Matriarchs always insist that broken rice bowls and chipped chopsticks are thrown away. They never allow chipped plates and tea cups to be used because it is one of the most widely acknowledged causes of businesses going wrong, losing money, and being cheated.

If you serve a guest tea from a teapot whose spout is chipped, if he knows anything about energy or feng shui, he will politely decline. He will also avoid drinking from a chipped teacup. This is because he will know that drinking from such a teacup will sap him of energy–he could get sick or lose vitality.

Do anticipate the problem by going through the crockery, vases, and ceramics that are in your home. Be firm with yourself. Throw away anything broken or chipped–even when the vase is expensive Waterford crystal and the plate is part of your prized collection of dinnerware. Discarding broken plates and utensils is one of the most important annual chores. Do this and you will be surprised at just how much damaged crockery lurks in your kitchen cabinet when you consciously look!

The Chinese see perfect crockery as promoting health, whereas chipped utensils sap vitality and bring bad luck.

Beware deadly killing energy inside the home 30

Develop sensitivity to the presence of hidden hostile energy inside your home. Hostile energy is killing energy–the kind that creates illness and disease, the kind that makes businesses collapse, and the kind that causes you to lose your job. Some of the more severe tragedies of life are caused by hidden sources of killing chi.

In recent years, with the rise in popularity of feng shui, many people have become more sensitive to these sources of shar chi–structural overhead beams, protruding corners, hostile art in the home, exposed knives, swords, and scissors–that can cause illnesses. Over the years, I have received thousands of emails giving me anecdotal evidence attesting to the effect of the simple disarming of killing energy inside the home. As their lives have become unburdened by less clutter, they have said how their physical health has improved, too.

So, camouflage that protruding corner, take down that hostile-looking piece of art, cover that overhanging ceiling, and block out all things sharp, triangular, and straight. Be very wary of deadly killing energy inside the home.

31 Overlapping energy fields

When you undertake energy work, be conscious of overlapping fields. There is seldom a single cause of good or bad luck, of good and bad vibes. In any space, there are multiple layers of energy fields and many of these overlap.

It is the dominant energy field in a house that has the strongest effect on the well-being of its residents. If it is benevolent, its effect is excellent. If it is hostile, its effect can be harmful. However, no one has all good or all bad luck. And it is the subtle energy fields that go deeper into your subconscious.

Life is never a canvas of absolutes. There are other fields of energy. Be aware that all energy fields are related to the human energy centers known as chakras. The energy of space vibrates in harmony with the chakras of the human body. So, depending on where you are in the development of your own spiritual awareness, you will tune into the energy that has the greatest meaning for you. Different people will experience varying degrees of comfort from a well-energized space. When you become familiar with chakra work, you will also develop acute sensitivity to energy–both negative and positive–that is in a space. The more spiritually attuned you are, the more sensitive you will be to overlapping energy fields. Those less familiar with chakras will notice the most dominant fields. Being in the latter group makes life a lot easier, as you will then have to tune in to the most dominant energy field,which is the one most relevant for reading the energy of the home.

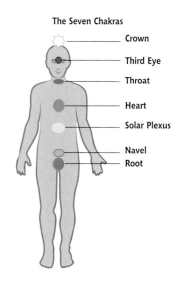

We respond to space, light and color in varying intensities. Intellectually we may be stimulated by the yellow of the walls,or by the red chairs. Everyone responds differently.

The Seven Chakras

Crown

Third Eye

Throat

Heart

Solar Plexus

Navel

Root

Bad vibrations emanating from furniture   32

All furniture has vibrations, particularly wood. There is something about wood that attracts chi so efficiently that wooden furniture is usually thick with accumulated energy. Usually the harder the wood is, the more that energy sticks to it. Antique furniture, usually made from very hard woods like teak, rosewood, and oak, tends to be thick with the energy of hundreds of years. Sometimes the energy emanating from furniture can be hostile, sad, or bad. It is vitally important to be aware of this, particularly if you are an antiques enthusiast.

A friend of mine, a serious collector, purchased an old wedding bed for his then unmarried daughter. It was a most auspicious and very rare piece, he said. It came from a very wealthy family. I wondered what a wealthy family was doing selling off a family heirloom like that. Later his daughter reached the age of 36–and was still unmarried. After her father passed away, I

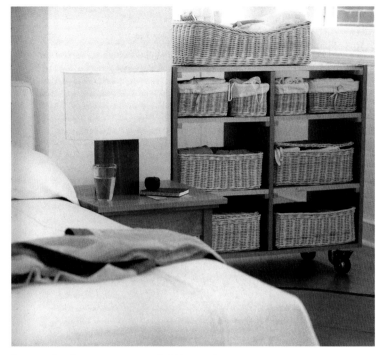

Even new furniture can carry uncomfortable energies.

attended his funeral and whispered to his daughter to get rid of the bed. "Otherwise, you will never get married," I told her. She put the bed up for sale and made a handsome profit–for it was indeed a masterpiece of craftsmanship. A month afterwards, she bumped into an old classmate she had not seen for many years. They rekindled their friendship and a year later married. In the same way that beds carry energy, so also do desks and chairs. When previously owned by someone powerful and cruel, their energy tends to be domineering and aggressive.

Consciously tune into the vibrations of your furniture. Who knows what feelings you may pick up–even when your furniture is new.

The Pussycat and the Tiger

A perfectly mild-mannered CEO I once knew invested in a stunning rosewood carved antique table and desk set that used to belong to a triad head in Shanghai during the early years of the twentieth century. I saw him literally transform before my eyes. He became steely and ambitious, and rose to take over the helm of the group for which he worked. Eventually he took equity control of the company. Gone was the quiet, unassuming man I once knew. I think that, for him, his chair and desk–complete with its carving of nine dragons–brought him good luck. Looking at him then and seeing a ruthless, ambitious man, I wondered how much of his new-found strength and energy came from his desk and chair set. Whether the antique set was good for him is a question of judgment and perspective.

33 Cleansing antique furniture with salt

When you bring home an old piece of furniture, you can cleanse it of lingering bad vibrations with salt, which dissolves negative energy and slices through ethereal dimensions to neutralize harmful, hostile chi.

Make a mixture of natural rock salt with natural sea salt in equal proportions. Synthetic chemical salt is ineffective–the strength and power of the earth and sea are needed, which is why natural salt must be used for this purpose.

Scoop a handful of the mixture into your hands and rub them together three times with an up and down motion. This sensitizes your palms. Then stroke the piece of furniture with them. Use a brushing motion, as if to flick off dirt from the surface of the furniture. Go around the surface of the furniture three times in a clockwise direction. Say cleansing mantras under your breath as you work. I always use my favorite mantra, "Om Mani Padme Hum," as it is an easy-to-remember yet powerful mantra of the Buddha of Compassion. The palms of your hands imbue your cleansing work with a great deal more power. Wash your hands thoroughly after this. If you do not like using your hands, use a damp cloth.

You can also give your old furniture a sunshine bath. Let it stand in hot sun for ten to fifteen minutes. If it is a desk, open the drawers, making sure the sunshine enters every corner of the desk. This is a powerful way to get rid of harmful old energy, and to revitalize it.

34 The energy of mirror reflections

Mirror reflections emanate strong energy. In advanced feng shui space cleansing work, experts use specially consecrated mirrors to absorb and capture all the bad energy from a room. Indeed, an easy method recommended by old monks from a temple in Singapore that is famous for the feng shui expertise of its abbot, is to simply place a round bronze mirror in a room said to be afflicted with bad energy.

This bronze mirror should be consecrated with a suitable mantra (a repeated prayer or blessing) used for blessing objects before it is placed in the room. Then, all bad vibrations will be sucked into the reflection and neutralized.

Bronze mirrors absorb any negative energy in a room.

Mirrors should always reflect brightness rather than darkness; clean spaces rather than cluttered spaces; and walls rather than doorways and long corridors. If you have a wall mirror in your home, look at it from various angles to make certain that it is always reflecting good, not afflicted, space. If you see that your mirror is reflecting anything inauspicious, such as a gloomy, cluttered corner, clear the space or cover the mirror so that it doesn't double the bad effects of the negative image. Mirrors reflecting auspicious features such as a beautiful lawn, flowers, or water feature outdoors are said to be bringing in the fresh revitalizing energy of nature.

Take extra care with corners 35

When it comes to negative energy building up, we should always take extra care with corners. For some reason, negative energy, cobwebs, and dirt tend to gravitate towards corners, and it is in them that one always sees the largest number of cobwebs and corpses of dead insects. Yet corners are also where the most benevolent chi also tends to settle.

The corner that is diagonal to the entrance door into a house is generally the most vital hot spot for assessing a home's energy quality. It is here that good chi flows and chi accumulations will bring a great deal of good luck to the residents of the home. Don't place sideboards and closets here, since doing so encourages the buildup of junk in the area. Do not put built-in cabinets here either, for the same reason. It is better to keep this place free and clear of clutter. Shine a bright light in this corner to encourage the flow of chi.

Take similar care with the corners of all the rooms in your house. Guard against the chi of corners growing stale and stagnant by making certain that the energy there remains constantly flowing. In addition to light, use sound for this purpose. Siting loudspeakers in corners is excellent for infusing them with yang energy. When the corners of rooms are clean and energized, the flow of chi is smooth.

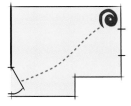
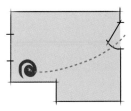

The corner that is diagonally opposite the door to a room should be full of good chi–so light this area brightly, do not use it for storage and always keep it clutter-free.

36   The flow of energy on stairwells

Be sure to assess the energy flowing up and down the stairwell in your home. Many people overlook stairways, not realizing that they occupy the space that connects the areas outside the house to the private quarters of the home. The chi of the stairwell must never ever be blocked. If it is blocked, make sure that you do something about it immediately.

Stairs and their surrounds must be kept clean for chi to flow smoothly. The area under stairs must be clutter-free, and no junk should be left on steps. This blocks the home's natural energy.

Of course, staircases can seem cramped simply because they are too narrow. Keeping the space well-lit should do a lot to alleviate this problem.

Stairwell chi can be empowered by hanging auspicious images on the wall alongside the staircase and keeping the whole area well-lit. I always recommend hanging a protective image at the bottom of the staircase and a "completion object" at the top, which symbolizes full potential.

This can be a painting of a harvesting scene, a fully opened flower, birds nesting or flying, ripened fruit, or something equally auspicious. Use your creativity and imagination.

Stairs and Clutter

Stairways also can become blocked when piles of boxes are left on the landing or cover the top of the staircase. Once my brother decided to go into the fan belt business and stocked up with boxes of fan belts, which he placed on the staircase simply because there was nowhere else for him to put them. During that period, he lost a great deal of money. Our parents lived in the same house then and they became very ill. Dad's illness was the more serious. He was diagnosed with high blood pressure and diabetes and he suffered a stroke, which left him very weak indeed. It was only after I insisted that my brother clear the stairs of his junk that our father recovered. With the chi flowing again, his health rapidly improved.

Releasing fresh energy into cramped spaces 37

At least once a month, or as regularly as your monthly routine allows you, try to let energy flow through all the cramped spaces of your home. Narrow hallways that are next to the staircase, for instance, will benefit tremendously from a flow of chi. These hallways are also conduits of chi and, although they may be small and cramped, the quality of the flow of chi is vital to the health of the house. So, once a month, open all the doors and windows to create a flow of fresh energy.

Newspapers and magazines

Never leave in corridors or near stairs stacks of newspapers and gossip magazines, because they tend to attract negative energy. Newspapers are horrible junk simply because they contain so many stories of crime, rape, war, and murder. All of this bad news crammed into your small hallway is not good energy. It is the same with gossip magazines. Throw them away after reading them. Never allow newsprint to pile up.

Glossy magazines containing beautiful products and beautiful people are nowhere near as bad as gossip magazines that carry unhappy news so much more often than the glossies. Keep all of your cramped spaces clear of these negatives.

Light

One of the best ways to take care of cramped spaces is to keep them well-lit. It is not necessary to have spotlights in them, but keeping a light on throughout the night attracts a higher density of yang energy. Use white rather than yellow light for such spaces.

If you have plants in your cramped spaces, do make certain that they are alive, clean, and healthy. Nothing looks sadder than dusty, wilting plants. Release fresh energy by moving the plants periodically.

Also, do change wall pictures and decorative hangings regularly. Otherwise, they grow tired, old, and sad. Do not let your pictures become frayed with age–they emit yin energy then.

If your walls look too dark, paint them bright, fresh white.

38 An eight-step revitalizing program

Decide to revitalize your home. After reading this book, make the decision to do so immediately.

1 Begin by making a list of all the things that are needed. Start with your own mind and inertia will fly out the window. Motivate yourself by visualizing your home with fresh energy that is clean, clear, and auspicious. Give yourself a time frame for this. Decide to do it all in one weekend or over four weekends, allotting yourself different rooms for different weekends.

2 Get organized. Spend ten minutes in each room with a notebook. List the things that need changing in every room, all the clutter you want cleared, and all the repair work you want to initiate. When you are finished, list the rooms in order of importance. Assign other members of the family to rooms if you want them to become involved. If not, assign yourself different days to address each room.

Getting started

3 Here's a tip: Start with the room that is of least importance to you, and leave the room that is most important until last. This way, you are sure to finish the job.

4 Convert one of your bedrooms into a workroom. This will be a halfway house room for you to place all the stuff you want to give away, repair, and sell.

5 Buy trash bags—ensure that they are strong and large, as you must throw into them all the things that you don't want. Clearing clutter is really very therapeutic—and it gets easier with practice. Do not cause yourself stress by being indecisive about what to keep and what to throw away. When in doubt, keep it. It will get junked in the next round of clearing in six months' time. Also, as you become better at this, you will find yourself becoming increasingly non-attached to possessions. Clearing clutter is not a one-time thing. Over time, you will find yourself doing it regularly—perhaps once or twice a year.

6 Revitalize your house with a fresh coat of paint at least once every three years. Get professionals in to do this if you can afford it. If not, then make a fun DIY (do-it-yourself) day of it. Paint your home room by room. Have fun with colors but if in doubt use white, which is very yang and suitable for all rooms. Give your home a proper scrub before you begin painting. Think of the layers of negative energy being scraped away and replaced with fresh new energy. The smell of fresh paint alone will make you feel better.

New light and air

7 This is one of the most effective ways to revitalize the energy of homes. Invest in a few extra lights—new lampshades, uplights, and light washes—and you will be amazed at how much warmer and brighter the energy in your house feels. Bring in sunshine energy with window crystals. Wash your curtains and hang faceted crystals in windows in order to draw in sunshine energy. It is very good to give your home or apartment a sunshine bath during the summer. Sunshine has the power to revitalize everything in your home—the walls, furniture, pillows, cushions, beds, carpets, and curtains. Sunshine energy brings fresh new yang energy into the home.

8 Let the wind flow through your house. Chi rides the winds. Bringing in the gentle breeze is inviting precious new chi into the home. It is therapeutic and very revitalizing.

Dejunking your life when you have moved on   39

It is amazing how much junk we collect. Our homes, and lives, collect it constantly. So does the mind. Junk-thoughts intrude upon our minds all the time. Try focusing on silence for a minute and you will see how hard it is. Thoughts flit in and out of the mind all the time–random thoughts enter our consciousness from various compart-ments of the memory bank, as if the brain is a machine running on auto-matic. It is the same with the home; in every corner of every room, there are random objects–articles of all kinds, small things, big things, fun things, useful things, junk things–that annoy and create stress for us. Our untidy rooms, stuffed closets, and piled-up desks can be so stressful. Usually we don't notice them, but, once we try to move on, or the thought of wanting to move on takes hold of us, the junk in our lives starts to overwhelm us–and often distracts and irritates us. Material and non-material junk is created by the mind.

Clutter is subjective–and books are a prime example. Giving away books you no longer want or need frees you from old ideas that may be holding you back.

Why clutter is subjective

Deciding whether something is junk is a purely subjective decision. Someone's prized possession is another person's junk. Something that means a great deal to someone else can mean absolutely nothing to you. So, dejunking your life means getting rid of stuff that you think of as junk. You are the one who must define what is junk.

Keeping precious items

Everything that gives you joy, makes you laugh, and inspires you–for whatever reason–is precious to you as it brings nourishing energy. Surrounding yourself with things you love, and which have meaning for you, will always strengthen you. This is

because the energy that vibrates around such objects is synchronized with yours.

Discarding bad-memory junk

Everything that causes you pain or anguish, makes you stressed out, annoys you, makes you feel inadequate, brings back unhappy memories, dulls your brain, and simply tires you out–in any way at all–is junk. All of it should be cleared and thrown away, never to annoy, disturb, or cause you stress ever again!

So when you have tired of anything–whether it is a book, newspaper, bag, clothes, decorative object, painting, furniture, curtains, or anything at all, however big or small, worthless or valuable, and it has lost its special meaning for you, lost its glitter... throw it out, sell it, or give it away!

40 Dejunking your life to make way for new things

Throwing out all the things that no longer have meaning or add to your sense of self is necessary if you want to create space for new developments in your life. I have discovered that this simple principle–creating a vacuum for opportunities to flow in–is even more powerful when used in conjunction with the feng shui directional compass. In feng shui, different directions signify different areas of life's aspirations; clearing out clutter in the eight corners of a room that coincide with the eight directions of the compass is a potent way of being very focused. So when you need to attract new luck into your life, look for junk that has accumulated in the corners of your home and also the room you occupy. Focus on these corners and combine the simple principle of creating space for new things by throwing out old stuff with the strategic placement of feng shui enhancers according to the easy rules of symbolic feng shui.

For example, if you want love and a new relationship, try applying these principles in the Southwest corner of your room and then place love symbols there, such as a pair of mandarin ducks. Dejunking any space leads to a dejunking of negative attitudes and aspirations that may have caused you grief. This is what is needed in order to create room for new experiences.

Green Light Enhances the Wealth God

The Chinese wealth god can be illuminated with green light to boost the wood element of the Southeast, the money corner.

In 1999 when my daughter graduated from university and came home to Malaysia, she needed a job, so I located the career corner of her bedroom (i.e., the north corner of her bedroom). It was occupied by a sideboard filled with her childhood junk. I cleared out toys, books, shorts, and other things that she no longer wanted and gave them all away. In that corner, I placed three large metallic coins to activate the element cycle with metal-producing water. The north being of the water element, I needed water to be produced in there, hence the coins. Just one month later, she was head-hunted by CISCO for their marketing department.

But what Jennifer really wanted to do was start her own business. So now I focused on her wealth corner, which was in the Southeast. I removed a bookshelf that had been placed there to store her childhood collection of toy ponies and dolls. In its place, I installed a green light to strengthen the growth energy of the wood element and in front of the light I placed the Chinese god of wealth.

A month later, Jennifer started a company called wofs.com on a small scale and, eight months after that, wofs.com attracted serious money when a multimillionaire offered her millions for a small stake in the company.

Clearing clutter is also a mental matter 41

Clearing the clutter is wonderfully liberating. This is because we rarely see our subtle tendency to put so much value on material support systems. When we realize how few of these material things really give us happiness, all the junk in our lives becomes more visible–and so we begin to understand that clearing clutter is also a mental matter.

Purifying the mind

I realized this when I did my first retreat at Kopan Monastery in Kathmandu. I decided I needed some spirituality in my life and signed up for a month's meditation course. The room assigned to me was so basic that I almost cried. It contained a bed, a table, and a chair. There was nothing decorative there; no perfume was allowed, no cosmetics, no radio, or books–just nothing. All I had were bare walls, basic necessities, and my own mind. Yet that month was the most life-changing experience of my life. Forced into survival mode, I turned inward and, helped along by the monks and nuns at Kopan, I discovered the world of my own mind. With nothing to distract me, I developed an increasing sense of awareness of my environment. I breathed in the intensely cold clean air, soaked in the rich feeling of the breezes.

Laundering thoughts

As I tuned my mind into me, I began to cleanse my mind of its impurities, afflictions, and negative thoughts. The process was both painful and cathartic. It was like washing dirty clothing.

When you first start to rub, all the dirt comes out and muddies the water, so you feel the pain, the aches, and the ego resisting –you get sick, you give in to self-pity, and you really want to give up. But the spirituality of the place and the meditation course helps you cope. So you hang in there until slowly the muddy water clears. Your mind develops acute sensitivity to the energy of time and space.

It was the most major dejunking I had ever done of my mind, and of my life. As a result, I felt lighter and brighter. Now I go back to Kopan at least once a year to clear away all the clutter that accumulates in my mind.

Clearing clutter is about mental attitude– understanding what is important to you in order to think clearly and live more simply.

42 Be sensitive to those you live with

Not everyone can appreciate the need for regular dejunking of his or her living space. And not everyone would agree on the definition of clutter. For many people, useless things that take up precious space are mere clutter–but what is clutter for one person may well be an object of affection to someone else.

Clearing clutter is easy when you live alone–when you are the sole judge of what is useless and what is precious. All you need to do is get started. Make a list; do it room by room. There is no need to consult anyone, no need to take account of anyone else's feelings and sentiments. Just block off a couple of weekends to give your home a complete overhaul.

Usually, however, clearing clutter is more complicated. Most people live with at least one other person, and most people live with other people who are totally unaware of the clutter around them. Over the years, these people have also developed a certain immunity to the negative energy–tiredness, lethargy, hostility, and blockages that lead to illness–that is generated by this kind of home environment.

The art of subtle persuasion

If you share living space with people who have this indifferent view about where they dwell, it can be tough for you to begin a regime of space-clearing. In such situations, be sensitive to those who live with you. Start small, clearing clutter a little at a time. Let them see how much nicer the energy of the home can be after it has been tidied, cleaned, and organized.

It is always safe to start with the living room, take extra time when altering bedrooms, personal desks, cabinets, and chests of drawers. Living rooms are the public areas of the home, so what is junk here is usually pretty obvious. When you start throwing away old newspapers and magazines, most people won't mind. But once you begin dejunking personal memorabilia, it is something else altogether–so remain sensitive to those with whom you live.

Many couples don't share the same preference for clutter-free interiors– what is junk to one partner may be a family heirloom to the other.

Not all clutter is bad

Distinguish good memorabilia from bad: think about what kind of memory an object evokes, rather than accepting it as a part of your personal history. Hold on to the good memories.

There are things in your life that you simply have no more use for, yet they continue to hold a small place in your heart– for whatever reason. These are things you are not yet prepared to let go of. In these cases, be soft on the so-called clutter–keep it, if only for another season, or until such time as you are ready to let go of it. News clippings of some past success, a faded picture of a long ago time, an old school report card, a birthday wish sent by some long-forgotten admirer whose words you loved, a childhood notebook, a lace blouse that brings back memories of good times– anything at all that would be thrown away under normal circumstances but which you still want–there is nothing and no one stopping you from keeping it. The object may be of no value, yet something holds you back from getting rid of it. Keep it, then, and realize that not all clutter is bad.

Trash or treasure?

There are always simple, even silly, objects in our lives that continue to carry positive energy simply by virtue of what they mean to us–happiness chi clings to things just as strongly as unhappiness chi. Energy works equally well either way. There is also a time dimension to energy. Who can say when something of great sentimental value becomes merely junk?

So accept that not all clutter is bad. There is no need to treat it like junk either. Honor things that once gave you joy. You will find that the memory of a moment of courage actually brings you courage when you need it, just as the memory of a moment of triumph can be intensely uplifting. There is no need to throw away objects that trigger such positive memories, which are reinforcements for our happiness.

44 Clutter that suppresses your energy

Do get rid of clutter that suppresses your energy. This consists of objects whose aura and chi are heavy, drip with hostility, and cause you angst each time you go near them. Usually clutter of this sort takes the form of furniture, paintings, or decorative items you have had to live with despite the intense negative vibrations you associate with them.

Sometimes it is simply the presence of one heavy object, associated with negative chi for the residents of a house, that is draining inhabitants of their energy. When such an object is removed, it is as if the house receives a new lease of life. And when energy inside it begins to move again, it almost always brings in good news.

Collections of artifacts can hold negative energy if they are associated with a difficult member of the family.

Time for a Change

I once had a girlfriend who had an old grandfather clock in the hall of her home that gave her the creeps each time she passed it. It had belonged to her husband's family and her mother-in-law had insisted that her eldest son keep the old clock to "remind him of his heritage." Over time, the heavy clock came to represent everything negative she associated with the old lady. Even long after her mother-in-law had passed on, the clock continued to be a major source of hostile chi for my friend.

When she told me this story, I was surprised about how agitated she became just describing the clock. "Get rid of it," I said, "It's obviously suppressing your energy and causing you real stress."

It had simply never occurred to her that she could sell it. She had lived with the clock for so long and it had established its presence so powerfully in her home that it had completely suppressed hers. My friend arranged to have it sent to an antique shop, where it later found a home with an energy that was more in tune with it.

The effect on my friend was amazing. With the grandfather clock removed from the hall, it seemed as if the chi of the old house began to flow once more, and she became energized. Her husband got a promotion, which she skillfully attributed to getting rid of the clock and the last time I saw her, she had also given her home a complete makeover.

Clutter that blocks energy 45

If you want your life to flow smoothly, clear everything that obstructs the flow of energy into and inside the home. Blocked energy vibrations of the home have a negative effect on its residents' well-being. Energy should move unimpeded from the entrance into the home and from one room to the next. When energy is blocked, your life becomes blocked–life becomes a struggle and success is hard to come by.

Where to begin

The foyer, hall, and staircase areas are most susceptible to clutter buildup. They are the home's energy conduits, so it is vital to keep them clutter-free.

The foyer Blocked foyers create a hostile environment that permeates the rest of the home, so clear this precious space of shoes, overcoats, and umbrellas. This allows the energy that enters by the main door to settle and accumulate before traveling through the rest of your home. Place a small side table here to hold everyday junk, and clear out your foyer daily. Keep walls and floors clean and uncluttered, and discard any tired paintings, posters, and other decorative objects. When you have created a clear, welcoming path through the foyer, vibrant good fortune chi can enter your home without hesitation.

Corridors and small halls These areas move the energy from room to room. Sure places to attract the buildup of clutter are sideboards, closets, and tables, where magazines, newspapers, junk mail, and forgotten unimportant possessions tend to get dumped. Clear these away. I am amazed at how fast junk piles up on tabletops and countertops. This type of clutter can be harmful when it piles up in halls and blocks the flow of chi. The solution for this is to move the furniture away, thereby creating a smooth path through which the chi can flow. Place a wastepaper basket here instead!

Staircases move the energy from one level of the home to the next, so they should not be stacked with clutter. Keep your stairways clutter-free, so that the flow of chi into the living quarters of the home is smooth. This greatly facilitates the replenishment of chi throughout the home.

Using Mirrors

Mirrors in halls or corridors should not reflect clutter as symbolically this doubles the negativity of junk. Use a rounded side table or closet to keep junk at bay; a round-leaved plant helps the smooth flow of chi at the corner of the alcove.

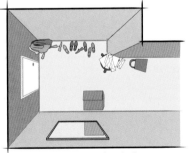

The mirror reflects the junk in the foyer.

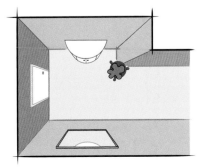

The mirror doubles the good chi of a junk-free foyer.

46 Paper clutter that affects mental well-being

There is a category of clutter that exhausts the spirit, distresses the mind, and clouds the judgment. This clutter piles up in workspaces and bedrooms, and it is normally associated with difficult and worrying issues. This is paper clutter–all your daily correspondence–that, if not dealt with affects mental well-being and triggers stress. It should never be allowed to pile up.

Many people leave unpaid bills, unfiled letters, faxes, and other documents unattended to for weeks and even months. This sort of paper clutter languishing on desktops, tables, and shelves, at home or at work, can be the source of much worry. The effect is subliminal, impinging on the subconscious mind and activating worry cells that may lead to migraine, stress, and tension. The physical body can be affected, and also the spirit.

So many important documents associated with the simple process of life–utility bills, tax filings, telephone notices–as well as unimportant junk mail come through the mail each day. Unconsciously we pile them up and in just a week the pile has degenerated into very harmful stress-inducing clutter.

Junk mail is junk

Invest in organizers and filing cabinets and develop the habit of throwing away junk mail the day it arrives. Junk mail is junk, yet so many of us hang onto catalogues we will never use, travel club news we will never refer to again, and, the bane of neatness freaks like me, organization newsletters and free magazines that are honest-to-goodness junk. Junk mail should be read when it arrives, and thrown away immediately.

Open all your other correspondence each day too, and set aside a few moments to do this. Discard the envelopes, and instantly file away important documents so that you never need to be affected by the stress caused by misplaced papers. The best way to clear clutter is to make certain that it never has a chance to pile up.

You can take turns with your spouse or assign a duty roster for doing this. In my home, this does not work, however. I have to be the one to clear the junk that comes through the mail each day–otherwise, it simply piles up.

Make a comfortable space in which you can sit calmly to deal with correspondence. Have a file to hand for papers you need to keep, and a wastebasket so you can immediately discard the real junk.

First clear out the real junk: unwanted stuff 47

Every home has its fair share of unwanted stuff – things that no member of the family wants, yet which no one gets around to throwing away. In this category of clutter are the obvious newspapers and out-of-date magazines, catalogs, and junk mail. There is also the less obvious clutter, and this is what can cause the energies of the home to fall out of sync, attract negative energy, or, worse, make energy stagnate and grow stale.

Here we are referring to electronic imple-ments that can no longer be used, such as broken-down stereo sets, radios, computers, irons, kettles, and air conditioners. Many people simply cannot accept that these conveniences of the modern age–what are generally referred to as white goods–do have a limited lifespan and do not last forever. When they break down, they should be thrown away or, if possible, taken to a recycling center.

Dealing with Hoarders

My husband kept his 1966 stereo system for years after it stopped working. He insisted on keeping an old refrigerator that had served us for twelve years, long after it had broken down. His closets were chock-full with suits and sports shirts bought decades ago. It is no wonder that his life went into a severe tailspin.

I decided to throw caution to the wind–and threw away all his hoarded junk. Interestingly, because what I cleared out was real junk, he never missed anything. That was the start of our good years. After that day, I systematically threw out everything that did not work, and renovated my home each year, corner-by-corner. I forced out all the junk that had piled up at the back of the house, in storerooms, and even in and around the outside bathroom.

This constant renovation allowed in precious new yang energy, as the throwing out of junk got rid of yin energy. Our life together just got better and better after that. We have been together now for over 35 years and he has accepted my fierce determination to throw out junk each year.

Indeed, once I realized how absolutely exhilarating this renewal process is, I began to look forward to clearing out our obviously unwanted belongings every year. I do this just before the lunar New Year, and I never cease to be amazed at the sheer volume of rubbish we manage to amass–and this is in spite of the clearing away I do each month. Newspapers, magazines, used batteries, and old clothes I sell to the junk man, who comes by regularly and pays us a few dollars for all our old possessions.

Old furniture, pictures and electrical goods such as radios can be real junk. If they are not of true sentimental value and, importantly, do not work, discard them immediately.

48 Next, clear out emotional junk: sentimental stuff

Items such as framed wedding photos need to evoke happy memories if you are to continue to keep them.

We all have sentimental stuff. This is what I term emotional junk: objects that tug at the heartstrings, love letters, pressed flowers, photos grown yellow with age, a song, a dress, an old carpet, a faded book–what price sentimentality?

There simply cannot be hard and fast rules about things that carry sentimental value for people who have lost loved ones along the road of life. Such objects have a life of their own, and the aura around them is usually bright and glowing. The energy attached to such objects is usually vibrant, kept alive and fresh by the sheer purity of love that was attached to them at the start.

Why should there be a need to throw them away then? No need at all. Objects that have emotional significance to only one person in the house nevertheless still have value in terms of the energy they emanate. Keep these objects. They are not junk. They are objects of affection, love, and devotion, and they can be revered as such simply because someone cares for them.

It is sentimental junk that no longer has meaning that should be discarded. Love letters from a past boyfriend who is now happily married to someone else, for instance, should have been thrown away long ago. The party dress worn to the Prom that ended in tears should have been given away to the church charity a decade ago. Faded photographs of less happy times should also be relegated to the trash can.

Choosing what to keep

If you must keep sentimental things, choose photographs of happy times, clothes that remind you of vibrant days, letters from dearly loved people who continue to be loved ones–and junk everything else. However, when you keep too many senti-mental objects, they tend to lose their meaning. If in doubt about whether to keep something, keep it for another year, and another year, until you reach a time when it really means nothing anymore. Then throw it away.

The clearing process can be very therapeutic, for in bringing back old memories, senti-mental objects from another time of your life can often give you new perspectives on your old feelings–and you can sometimes wonder why you felt the way you did so many years ago. When cathartic realizations like this occur, they can be very healing indeed, allowing you to let the past rest, and acknowledge that you are ready to move on.

Clearing clutter awakens chi   49

Clearing clutter is the best antidepressant there is. This is because stale, stagnant air that usually sticks to untouched, unmoved junk in the home often makes the surrounding chi heavy, creating vibrations that make you feel depressed. Each time I meet someone assailed by the blues who seems set on a downward spiral of depression, I know that part of the reason is that the energy of their surrounding space is too heavy for them and is weighing them down.

Beating the blues

Making the effort to awaken the chi of their living space by moving stuff around–not necessarily junk, but just stuff that has somehow piled up over the years–is usually so effective in forcing their own internal chi to also move that the result is a lifting of their spirits that is amazing to watch and experience. A certain lightness of being begins to pervade the atmosphere, not unlike the effect that an hour's work-out at the gym has. Clearing clutter engages both

the physical and mental dimensions of the self. It is hard work physically, but it is also very relaxing. As all those trash bags pile up, it is as if, in freeing the chi around you, you are also lifting your own spirits. Depression flies right out of the window and, as you finish your clear-out, a genuine sense of renewal comes over you.

Clearing clutter and storing what you keep effectively brightens the chi of your home.

Attuning to the clearing process   50

It is important to attune yourself to the clearing process. The act itself is a departure from a normal kind of day. It is a departure from routine, and the mind gets a creative jolt that is not unwelcome. When the mind focuses on the process of dejunking physical space, it automatically goes into cleansing mode. This means that what you do in the material space around you often imprints itself on the subconscious mind as well, so that tuning in to the clearing process creates many wonderful side effects. This is not just shrugging off garbage from your life and mind in a subconcscious way, but also the mind

goes into an organizational mode. There is an instant when the mind tunes into what can be done to simplify the cleansing process in the future and a certain awareness of space takes root.

Every time you clear out your clutter, it will take you less time to do so and the whole process will feel increasingly natural. Each time it will become easier, but the important thing is to start, for, once you experience its benefits, you will want to do it again and again. This is how the mind reacts, adapts, and contributes to any beneficial activity.

51 Clear junk that blocks doors and doorways

Keep entrances on both sides of doors free of junk, and good fortune chi will flow unimpeded into your life. Projects will move along smoothly, and relationships will bring you the joy associated with smooth sailing.

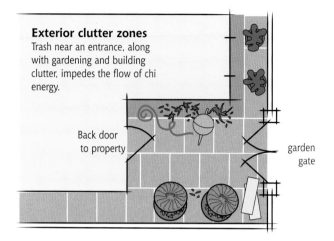

Exterior clutter zones
Trash near an entrance, along with gardening and building clutter, impedes the flow of chi energy.

Back door to property

garden gate

Types of door affliction
The doorway is where you, your spirit, and the spirit of your space and home move in and out. This flow of chi must never be blocked, afflicted, or tainted.

Blocked flow-paths If this flow-path is blocked, your life also is blocked. Nothing works, nothing moves. Relationships flounder. People get stuck in ruts in their jobs. Upward mobility comes to a halt. When the path into the home is blocked, opportunities dry up. When the path from the home to the outdoors is blocked, you become imprisoned inside your home. Your social life dries up. You lose vitality, vibrancy, and energy.

Afflicted entrances This happens when junk piles up to the extent that it poisons the energy of the doorway. Entrances afflicted in this way may cause the home's residents to suffer illness, lose money, and experience one piece of bad luck after another. Afflicted entrances are akin to being attacked by poison arrows. It is absolutely vital to get rid of the source of this kind of affliction: clean both sides of the door, and clear away the junk near it.

Protecting Your Door from Tainted Energy

An entrance may be tainted by energy that has slowly piled up and turned poisonous through the passage of time, or by energy that has been brought in via incoming furniture, people with bad feelings, or objects brought in innocently by residents. Entrance ways are especially vulnerable to incoming negative energy, and it is for this reason that feng shui experts always recommend placing the images of protective celestial creatures near them.

Because of this, you will find that many Chinese abodes even today place Chi Lins, Fu dogs, Pi Yaos (illustrated here) and even traditional door gods at the entrances of their homes. These are

thought to offer a certain amount of protection against incoming negative energy. If you have these protective symbols in your home, do make certain they are never overwhelmed by a pile of clutter around them.

In the past I have visited a number of shops whose protective Fu dogs, positioned to guard the doorways, were literally buried under a pile of boxes and other junk. The owners wondered why their suppliers were cheating them. However, as soon as their entrances were cleared of all the rubbish that had piled up, their problems with their suppliers immediately cleared as well.

Remove junk obstructing corridors and halls   52

Make a special effort to ensure that the careless buildup of junk never blocks the halls and corridors of your home. These are vital conduits of chi flow and it is really important to let the chi move unobstructed through these areas. One way to guard against the buildup of junk is not to place tables or sideboards in hallways and corridors. By making sure that there are no convenient tabletops and storage spaces here, you will be helping these vital conduits of energy to stay tidy and clear. Think of corridors and staircases as the veins and arteries of your body, making precious energy flow inside you.

Halls need good energy flow, but the chi must meander rather than rush. Placing an item of furniture, or an inspiring picture, at the landing helps the chi pause and create a calm and unhurried ambience.

To help the flow of chi along, it is always a good idea to keep hallways well-lit and walls and carpets there clean. Most of the time, these places do not have access to natural light so that one has to make a conscious effort to ensure that chi there does not become stale.

Using Light and Music

Some time ago, I visited someone who lived alone in a London town house. Her home felt very narrow and constricted. Directly facing the entrance door to her home was a staircase, with a long, thin hall running to the side of it. This hall–deep, dark, and gloomy–was also blocked by a coatrack which stood by the stairway. It seemed as if the many coats hanging off it had been there for a very long time. In fact, it gave me the creeps.

Now the owner suffered from severe loneliness. She had attended one of my lectures and something about her air of resignation, and her defeated expression, had tugged at my heartstrings. I had agreed to follow her home. When I saw her home, it was clear to me that something could easily be done to bring back vitality into this lady's life. She was wonderfully agreeable when I suggested that she throw away the cumbersome coat-rack, as well as the coats. She had long outgrown them, yet even through the change of seasons, it had never occurred to her to pack them away. Now she donated them to the local charity and immediately felt a rush of exhilaration from having liberated the hall. Next, she brightened the whole foyer area by installing lights. She also placed a loudspeaker there to enhance yang energy with piped-in music, as I told her that this was one excellent way to attract more people into her life.

That was several years ago. The last time I met her, she was working part-time for a local Buddhist meditation center. Her social life has become very busy and her life has taken on new meaning. She looked so radiant and fulfilled.

53 Managing clutter on tabletops

It's a good idea to direct your attention, on a regular basis, to the tabletops of your home. Why? Because tabletops become covered in junk so fast that it's incredible. Coffee tables, kitchen counters, work tables, cabinet surfaces, dressing tables, and office desktops all collect it. Any elevated surface will invite you to place your bags, groceries, files, and envelopes upon it–so it is absolutely necessary to devise a method for keeping tabletops at least reasonably clear of junk.

Anything empty symbolizes scarcity

First, differentiate between different types of junk. You must decide whether something belongs elsewhere or should be thrown away. I am particularly sensitive to empty containers. Bottles, jars, boxes, and tubes that are empty should be thrown away. There are few things more harmful than empty containers exposed on tabletops. They symbolize emptiness and are the opposite of abundance.

Defining the function of tables

Note the function of your tables. Do they hold lots of permanent objects, such as framed pictures, table lamps, books, and plants? Most people's homes have tabletops like this, but often they are so full that there is no room for temporary items such as invitations. A good approach to reducing clutter is to choose decorative objects and place them

When you bring a new table into your home, decide what you want it to hold and stick to it, rather than wait to see what it accumulates.

well on your "permanent" table, leaving no room for junk, and allocate another table for temporary items.

Conventional wisdom suggests that it really does not matter how full your tables get, so long as you are aware of the need to clear them occasionally. As long as energy never remains stagnant in a particular area, clutter will not be present long enough to become a severe problem.

I like using my tabletops to display feng shui enhancers that attract good luck into the various corners of my home. So I keep my tables relatively full but neat and clear of clutter.

It is best to display full bowls of pots as they attract abundant chi.

Keep your kitchen clear as all junk there is bad 54

The buildup of junk in the kitchen can be quite dangerous. This is because bad energy can seep into the food you eat. Cooked food is not as susceptible to absorbing yin chi (which can cause illness) as cold food is, since it is already yin. If you are a salad-and-sandwiches person, do ensure that your kitchen stays reasonably free of yin energy, which emanates from kitchen clutter.

Revitalizing your kitchen

You need to dejunk your kitchen as often as possible to avoid this harmful build-up of yin chi. Below are essential practices:

Clean the refrigerator Do this once a month, so that leftover food does not get lost in the back of it and rot into poison. Do the same for the cabinets that hold grocery goods. For instance, people have a nasty habit of ignoring canned food for so long that it turns bad before they notice. The same thing happens with exotic sauces and seasonings that become harmful junk as they degenerate in half-open bottles and containers.

Check out cookware In the kitchen, all physical junk is bad and should be thrown away. Included in this category are not merely stale food and foodstuffs, but also broken plates, cups, and bowls. Cooking pots and pans also cannot last forever and, once defective,

they should be replaced; don't buy a new frying pan and keep the old one with its scratched Teflon surface–or that worn-out, ugly coffee maker that you have already replaced with a brand new model.

Double-check trash cans So make sure to clear the garbage regularly and to throw away rotting food. Also, clear the cat litter and make sure that kitchen goldfish bowls are kept clean. I have seen untidy, dirty kitchens ruin more marriages and cause more heartache than I care to tell. Among all the rooms of the home, this is the place that is most vulnerable to the buildup of yin energy, so treat all physical junk here as bad and get rid of it.

A truly clean and well-ordered kitchen keeps energy-sapping yin chi at bay.

55 Annual cleanups of closets are a must!

Your closet should be a source of joy and inspiration since it is the place you go each morning to prepare yourself to start the day. I place great importance on having a closet filled only with adornments that I love and clothes that fit me and are immediately wearable in colors, cuts, and styles that I like at any moment in time.

Alas, for most people, this is an ideal situation. Many fill their closets with clothes they do not like and seldom wear, and ones that do not fit. This is an ailment from which many of us suffer. It took me thirty-five years to get my act together on this one.

I realized how much stuff I had hanging in my closet only when I had to move house. I was leaving Hong Kong to return home to Malaysia and the packers had come to help me ship my belongings there. My clothes alone filled half a container. I looked in dismay at dresses I had forgotten, suits I had long since thought had been thrown away, and loads of accessories, scarves, belts, and shoes. It was then that I discovered I was just a hoarder, clinging to things I had disdainfully discarded as last season's fashion yet was so stupidly attached to them that, instead of throwing them away, I had simply stuffed them deeper into my dresser and closet.

The eighty-twenty rule

Since then I have forced myself to spring-clean my closets every year. I discard about twenty percent of my wardrobe–clothes, shoes, bags, and accessories–to make space for new things.

I am now more careful when shopping. Now I only buy clothes and accessories I absolutely love, in colors that I am sure to wear, in sizes that are certain to fit me the next year, and in cuts that make me feel comfortable. I also consciously buy half the clothes I think I need. And I never ever buy anything in duplicate, no matter how much I love the style. Now my closet space is a lot smaller, hence easier to keep well-organized.

Go for fewer clothes that really suit you rather than hoards of "just-in-case" items that you never wear.

Treat bedrooms as sacred spaces 56

Keep your bedroom free of clutter for peaceful, restful sleep. Treat this area as if it is a sacred space, since this is where you spend all of your sleeping, subconscious time. It is where you leave the conscious world, and go into another dimension. Here is where you dream dreams, and let yourself go. Here is where you rest, cocooned from the world. So keep this space sacred and special.

Keep the energy of the bedroom free from energy that is negative, harmful, stale, or hostile–so throw out things that make the energy turn sour. Instead, place only things you love in your bed-room, things that make you feel pampered and beautiful.

Keep the bedroom bright, clutter-free, and comfortable.

Practical Tips

1. Don't store clothes high on elevated shelves in your bedroom. This is a bad idea because they create heaviness above the sleeping level. Store your winter wardrobe in a store-room and keep all of your suitcases in another room.

2. Keep all exercise equipment, bikes, and wall mirrors out of the bedroom. Your place of rest is not your gym.

3. Make sure that all work-related junk is kept away from the bedroom. Do not have a work desk here, so that you eliminate the danger of work-junk piling up inside the bedroom. Keep computers and telephones out. Let children have a special study room, rather than a desk in their bedroom. If there are insufficient rooms in your house for this, try to place the desk a little away from the bed so that junk that builds up on the desk does not affect the sleeping child.

4. Keep all dirty clothes inside a laundry basket. Nothing is more yin than dirty clothes, and the energy permeates any room pretty fast.

5. Do not place junk under, over, or beside a bed. Keep beds clean at all times.

6. Keep all doors clear of junk so that they open and close smoothly.

7. Never hang questionable art on the walls of your bedroom. Refer to the section on art to make certain you never hang anything that can attract bad luck.

8. Keep windows clear of clutter. Curtains can be left open or closed at night, but it is advisable to let the light flow in once the sun shines. Nothing brings in better yang energy than morning sunlight.

57 Discard junk in storerooms, attics, and basements

Clearing clutter becomes a complete exercise when you systematically discard junk that lies hidden in storerooms, attics, and basements.

Four types of junk to let go of

You will find much that should be thrown away in these natural storage areas of the home. Below are four areas to begin with—so tune your mind into letting go of junk, and make a start.

If it's broken and not collectable, it's junk.

Junk collections These range from the sublime to the ridiculous—fans, plastic ducks, matchbooks, toy monkeys, carved horses, ceramic toads, stamps, and stones. Almost every kind of collection mania you can think of has been enjoyed by someone somewhere. If you have a collection that is no longer on display in your living room, and has found its way into your attic or basement, you have moved on. These objects no longer mean much to you, so why not arrange for them to go to someone else who will enjoy them? Kept in storage rooms, their energy simply stagnates.

Books and magazine junk makes energy grow very stale, as they represent dated information—so discard immediately.

Photographs are a third kind of junk. Take some time to go through them. Throw away those that don't bring back pleasant memories and definitely get rid of those that recall negative emotions. Keep only photographs that bring a smile to your face, not tears to your eyes. Then remount them. Give them fresh new energy so that they become a source of strength and love for you. Photographs are very much a part of your family. Transform those that you keep into things that are genuinely precious.

Broken equipment Everything in the basement that is broken or has been discarded should be junked. Get rid of it all—stereos, TV sets, old computers, exercise equipment, hair dryers, lawn mowers, odds and ends for the car, plus all boxes, bottles, and other containers for which you have no need.

It is impossible to list everything that should be discarded from your storage rooms. In everyone's life there are things such as unwanted presents, things we dislike, and things that no longer work that we keep, out of misguided feelings of guilt or in the hope that they can be repaired some time. But, believe me, if you don't like it today, or don't need it today, chances are you will never like it or need it.

Turning Over a New Leaf

My father's collection of National Geographic magazines, lovingly bound over the years, choked my mother's energy long after he had died. Each time she spied them on the shelves, they would make her so remorseful that the only solution was to help her make a clean break with them. It was not until I had separated her from them that she recovered from the spiral of depression that had gripped her and regained her vitality.

Keep purses and handbags clear of clutter 58

Dejunking unwanted stuff from your life to enhance the space around you is incomplete without also clearing the junk that lies under the pile of stuff in your bags and purses. A woman's handbag is the ultimate store of junk–such as receipts, credit card slips, odd pieces of paper, business cards, keys, old lipsticks, reminder note-books, pens, pencils, and heaps of personal memorabilia like letters and photographs. Within just one week, a handbag can bulge with a truly amazing collection of assorted clutter.

It is an excellent idea to empty your personal handbag once a week to get rid of unwanted rubbish. I do this all the time and never cease to be amazed at how much stuff I have inside my bag which I do not need. In recent years, I have begun to need yet larger bags. What with cell phones and palm pilots, orga-nizing one's life has not become easier in this high-tech era. For many, the palm pilot has not made the personal organizer or the diary redundant. We still need all of these personal support systems to keep track of our days.

Therefore, clean out your bag regularly. Get rid of soiled money and don't let the amount of coins you carry become too heavy.

To attract wealth, keep your wallet or coinpurse free of old tickets, notes, and general clutter.

A red purse for prosperity

A clean purse is very auspicious. The best color for a purse is bright red, which keeps it constantly energized with yang chi. Place three coins tied together with red string inside it to attract money, and never let your purse become tainted with soiled money. If you can, keep a dollar bill from a rich person's pocket. This will create wealth energy for you.

Dejunk unwanted files from your computer 59

Dejunking your mind and your space should also extend to your computer, which stores so much of our rubbish these days.

Make it a habit to regularly dejunk your computer. It is better for the running of your computer and keeps it in good condition. You will find it really easy to trash ninety percent of your electronic mail, for example, because so much of it is junk anyway. But do make certain that old emails are really thrown away and not simply lying in your trash folder. This can be likened to lit-tering the basement or attic of your home until you get around to clearing out all the unwanted debris.

Once a month, spend an hour or so determinedly deleting all of your unwanted pictures, files, memos, and emails. You will find that doing this is not only good for your computer; it feels good for you too as you are symbolically deleting unwanted information and freeing up your brain space. Don't forget that doing this extends the principles of clearing clutter to the tools of the twenty-first century.

60 Keep your work desk clear of junk

Your work desk should be kept reasonably clear of junk. If yours is a working style that requires piles of files and papers on your desk, then at least make certain that the mountain of files and paper is not placed directly in front of you, blocking your view. This will only cause your view of work itself to become blocked. Do not place piles directly behind you either, as this means you will always feel weighed down with work. Instead, keep files and papers to your left in order to simulate dragon chi.

Desk drawers also have a way of becoming clogged with a broad variety of things that cross a working person's daily life at the office. Do not let these things choke up your career. A congested desk will create traffic jams in your working life. Instead, keep the chi moving, especially the chi on your desk. Let nothing stagnate. If you have fresh flowers on your desk, for instance, change the water daily and throw out wilting flowers, as there can be nothing more damaging to your working life than dying blooms.

Always keep any decorative items on your desk to a minimum. Framed photographs, crystals, pen holders, executive games, feng shui enhancers, and so forth, should all be kept to a sensible number. If these things threaten to overwhelm the tabletop, there is no space left for new opportunities to come in.

You may keep your desk free of clutter, but be aware of shelves taking the strain. Their edges also create "poison arrows", a type of negative chi.

Keep books, diaries, and files to the left of your chair to activate energetic dragon chi.

Women should keep important items in the left-hand drawer.

Men should keep important items in the right-hand drawer.

Develop concentration to detect negative chi   61

If you make a real effort, you can eventually develop a sense for negative energy. This sense arises at first as a feeling of detached unease, which eventually expands into a broader awareness. Relatively quickly, you will be able to differentiate between different types of negativity and whether it may be hostile, lethargic, or sick.

The key to developing your awareness of energy is determined by how well you can concentrate. Concentration creates alertness to other realms of consciousness and parallel dimensions of existence. But concentrating for even just a few minutes is difficult unless one also generates a strong desire to master the mind and disallow distraction.

Negative energy is easier to detect than positive energy. This is because negative energy causes negative emotions and memories to surface. Negative energy almost always engenders feelings of discontent and dissatisfaction. The influence of surrounding energy on the way we act and react to people is very powerful; therefore, when

If you find it difficult to concentrate at first, try gazing into candlelight and focusing on the movement of the flame. This increases your receptivity. Extinguish the flame, then try the exercise outlined here.

you systematically transform negative energy in your living space into positive energy, it will alleviate many of your ills, and lighten so much of all that makes you unhappy.

How to Tune in to Your Surroundings

1. Start by closing your eyes and imagine you are shutting out all visual distractions. Focus on the intangible invisible energy of your surroundings. When thoughts intrude, push them gently out of your mind, or let them drift away like clouds without dwelling on them.

2. Allow your more receptive, subconscious mind to sense the subtle variations of energy in space, of which your conscious

mind is not yet aware. Let them seep into your conscious mind from your subconscious while you are in a state of focused concentration.

3. You will notice these subtle energy changes, initially, through the way your moods shift. Do you feel irritable, impatient, angry, depressed, or engulfed in a peaceful state of quiet and calm?

Become aware of what kind of mood your surroundings inspire in you. Feel the energy of the space.

4. Open your eyes and make a mental note of your feelings during your tuning in. If you like, write this in a journal—date your entry, as this will be a useful benchmark as you proceed with dejunking and the energy of your spaces transforms.

62 Counter negative energy with new chi

Negative energy is best countered by bringing new energy into a living space. New energy is young, fresh, and has great vitality; it replenishes any home, keeping the chi inside it robust and growing.

Bringing in new chi
Chinese Taoist masters always stress that the relationship of yin and yang must be assessed according to their strength and vigor. It is important to sense whether yang energy is young or old so that one can differentiate between strong yang or dissipating yang. Yang energy that has grown old is exhausted and will turn into yin unless it is reinvigorated and given new energy.

Move your furniture around at least once a year to keep the chi moving. I do this two weeks before the lunar New Year (in early February); you can do this before western New Year or during the Christmas holidays. It is amazing how much strength I feel flowing into my body each January when I start this major house re-energizing exercise. As well as cleaning in every corner of your home, include the rituals and cleansing ceremonials that appeal to you, for they generate positive shifts of the intangible forces that enhance the energy of your home.

Remodel and redecorate your home every three to four years. Sometimes it is enough to just clean and repaint the walls. Other times more serious renovations, in accordance with changing Flying Stars, may be undertaken (see Tips 11–14). This can involve placing a water feature in a certain corner, changing a door into a window, or expanding a room because favorable chi is flying into it. Houses always feel so good after a well-planned feng shui renovation. It causes a rush of new chi into the home, which has the most revitalizing yang effect.

Light and color bathe a home in fresh new energy. Paying attention to windows also brings in yang energy that creates vitality in your living space.

Stifled, locked-in energy   63

Negative energy can be stifled when it is trapped inside homes and offices. These are buildings whose windows and doors are seldom opened to let the air in.

In the tropics, where temperatures are so high that people live in air-conditioned homes and rooms, travel in air-conditioned cars, and work in air-conditioned offices, some people never breathe fresh air. Over time, those who have no regular regime of exercise grow sick from breathing stagnant air day after day. People in this condition are badly in need of new chi.

Breathing yang chi is a luxury for city people

In temperate countries, it is the intense cold of the winter months that causes homes to stay locked up tight, but the result is the same. The chi within these homes is recycled and so such places cry out for new energy. This is a problem that afflicts city folk, as a result of which an entire range of new ills and diseases have been discovered in the past fifty years... all caused by people living in excessively yin spaces.

Tune in to the chi of your living or working space. Consider whether there has been too much recycling of stale air in it. Try opening the doors and windows and feel the energy shift instantly. The simple act of opening doors and windows in the home, to suck in air and wind from the great outdoors, has a

The high windows bring in yang energy, but this is stifled by the yin of the deep-pile rug which, when the windows are closed, creates a claustrophobic environment.

fabulous revitalizing effect upon it. Make the effort to revitalize enclosed spaces like this at least once a month, if not more often. You will find that you need to have at least two openings (doors or windows) to create a flow of chi in an area. Simply keeping one door open will not bring in chi from the outdoors. You must facilitate this flow of energy, and then you will feel the gentle wind and breezes breathing new life into your living space.

Do this during the morning hours before your environment becomes polluted.

64 Removing negative chi coming from neighbors

Many people suffer from negative chi coming from next door or across the hall. When you have nice, friendly neighbors, the energy coming from them toward you is positive and reinforcing, but when they are unfriendly, the energy will be negative. This can be very harmful for city dwellers. When neighbors send you negative chi on a regular basis, you are sure to succumb to it unless you tune in to it, realize what it is, and then do something to divert or dissolve it.

Dealing with hostile chi

Hostile chi from neighbors may be the comparatively harmless chi of frivolous gossip and small-minded envy or, at other times, it can be merely annoying. For instance, your neighbor may have a house full of screaming children who disturb your rest, break your things, and annoy you with their loud antics. Overcoming this is easy. Just place a large urn of water with a wide mouth and a narrow base between yourself and them.

The mirror cure If the energy being sent your way is bitter or hateful, or something more sinister, you may want to counter it with stronger measures. There are many

Still water is yin water. If you have noisy neighbors, place a water urn by your adjoining wall or fence to soak up the sound.

different ways to protect yourself. For centuries, the Chinese have used a round mirror encircled by trigrams arranged like the Yin Pa Kua symbol. This is really powerful and harmful, as it bounces back bad energy and magnifies it a thousandfold. This is not necessary, however–instead, you can use a round mirror of about twelve inches (30 cm) in diameter. If there is any clutter near the wall or fence that you share with your neighbor, do remove it. When you keep the conduit of chi that flows between you and your neighbors neat, and the dividing wall or fence is decorated with loving images such as birds and hearts, you will find that a great transformation takes place. Enmity can be transformed into friendship.

The Bell Cure

Hanging bells in a way that traverses the divide between you and your neighbor can effectively disperse incoming negative energy. The only problem with using bells is that you may inadvertently magnify any existing quarrelsome chi. Also, when quarrelsome Flying Star aspects are present, using bells may make things worse. Because of this, I prefer to use the mirror cure, supplemented with an urn of still water.

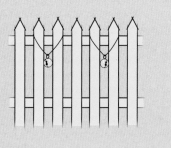

Getting rid of left-over chi from previous tenants 65

Another kind of negative energy is that left over from previous occupants of a home. Before signing the lease on any place, no matter how temporary your stay there, do ask about the history of previous occupants.

Chi and illness

Negative chi lingers in homes formerly occupied by people who were ill, especially sickness of the terminal or mental kind; these illnesses tend to generate very sticky chi. The walls, floors, and ceilings retain left-over attitudes, unhappiness, and pain, which should be cleared in order to allow in new energy that will dilute and weaken old energy.

Chi and anger

Negative chi of the angry, aggressive kind can also be left behind by past occupants whose lives were consumed by anger, bitterness, and violence. These are strong emotions that inadvertently become stuck on the walls and ceilings of a home. Sometimes they are so strongly stuck that no amount of scraping and repainting can get them off. This is the case when a home has been closed most of the time, especially one with heavy drapes and dark-colored walls. Yin chi captures and stores the spirit of anger and unhappiness very well.

When negative chi has seeped into the spirit of a home in this manner, it must be released. Releasing it is not difficult. It is not hard to cleanse spaces of their left-over energy, regardless of how strong the negative energy is.

There are powerful spatial purification techniques or cures that anyone can use to sweep away old negative energies. These involve the use of metal objects, including bells, cymbals, and singing bowls. When specially made from seven types of metal, to represent the seven chakras of the human body, these space-purifying implements can be very powerful in making negative energy disperse. Look for these feng shui space-clearing tools and learn different methods of striking them so that their sounds absorb negative things. It is the harmonics of metal and wood, and metal on metal, that makes them so powerful.

When looking for a new home, watch out for signs of neglect such as peeling paint. Never be deterred by a home's history, but be prepared to carry out space-clearing rituals to disperse old negative energy.

66 Remedies for people living near a burial ground

If your home or apartment house is located near a burial ground, it is a good idea to cleanse your home regularly with incense. This also serves as a gesture of offering to wandering spirits who may be passing by your house, ensuring that they do not cause imbalances to its energy fields. Homes located near cemeteries are vulnerable to what is known as yin spirit formation, an affliction that often brings illness to children or those whose astrological timing is low and weak.

The Chinese are especially sensitive to this kind of affliction and often combat it with fire-energy cleansing, which makes use of incense and smoke. It is believed that smoke from holy fragrant incense that is placed on burning coal keeps yin spirits away from your home.

Taking smoke from incense burning in a container around rooms in a clockwise direction helps drive away the kind of chi that brings sickness to the occupants of a house. Do this three times. If you know some holy mantras, simultaneously chant them as you walk around the rooms

Another thing that draws in yang energy is candlelight. Gently pass three lit candles (red ones are best) across the front door of your home three times, in a clockwise direction. Extend the candles high above your head three times and then near the bottom of the entrance three times.

If your home is right next door to a burial ground, painting the wall that adjoins it red is a good way of balancing the energy there.

67 Remedies for those living near a hospital

Incense smoke soaks up the yin chi associated with illness.

If you live near a hospital, you are in close proximity to yin spirits. This is because hospitals are where the yin chi of sick (and dying) people accumulates, and this is not healthy for yang living abodes. It saps the vitality of your home. Even apartment houses and mansions on land where a hospital used to be are said to be afflicted with left-over energy. This energy can be so yin as to cause residents illness and problems.

I know some wealthy Malaysians and at least two Hong Kong millionaires who bought stunning apartments in the Kensington area of London. The land on which the whole apartment complex stood used to be a hospital. Without exception, the residents I knew suffered major setbacks within a year of moving in, losing on business investments made in the UK, and becoming severely ill.

Fire energy, in the form of incense smoke, absorbs yin chi and dissipates it, and so is an effective way to balance the yin emanating from hospitals or hospital land and also police stations, abattoirs, and other places where there is death, sickness, and dying energy present. Many Chinese, who observe space-cleansing rituals purify their homes with incense smoke each Friday evening just after sunset. A more permanent solution is to keep your place well-lit. Painting the wall that is facing the source of yin energy a bright red is also a powerful cure.

Protection against an intimidating building   68

Negative energy can also emanate from excessively large buildings that directly face the front of your house. In this situation, the sheer strength and power of the buildings' life force swamp the vitality of your home. The effect is similar to facing a mountain. In the old days, facing a big mountain that was less than one li away (about two-thirds of a mile, or one kilometer) was described as "confronting the mountain" something which no right-thinking man would dream of doing. In city landscapes, buildings are interpreted as having energy similar to that of mountains, although of course the energy of buildings is tiny compared to that of mountains. Buildings are young, usually being less than fifty years old, while mountains contain the accumulated chi of thousands of years.

Practical remedies

While the tangible effect of facing a building is similar to facing a mountain, it is easier to overcome the intangible negative chi that is emanating from a building. Using mirror cures for this are often recommended in feng shui, but it is also possible to tap the energy of the building rather than to fight with it. If you can, change the direction the

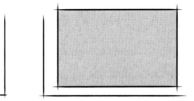

If your home stands in the shadow of a larger, intimidating building, diffuse the energy racing toward your home by leaving decorative spaces in your wall.

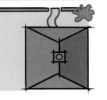

Use trees and a meandering path to reduce the feeling of energy imbalance if your home is oppressed by a larger building.

house is facing, so that the building may be used as a support for its back. If this is not possible, then build a solid wall in front of the building and hang a row of wind chimes, bells (see Tip 64), and anything else made of metal in front of it. This reduces and slows down the chi coming from across the road towards your house. Also place some openings in the wall so that the chi coming from across the road will slow down and then filter through to your home in small doses.

Wind chimes and bells are excellent for controlling mountain energy, and they are also very efficient for overcoming any negative chi that may be emanating from across the road. In protecting and nurturing the energy of your home, don't be intimidated. When in doubt, it is better to adopt a posture of submission rather than confrontation. This attitude is really excellent and useful when practicing feng shui as well.

69 When your family falls ill, use metal chi

Sickness in the home is very often due to intangible forces caused by what in feng shui are referred to as the Sickness Stars. These usually affect young children under the age of twelve and also the older people of the household because they tend to be weaker and thus more vulnerable and sensitive to changes in energy. When family members fall ill, the best cure for them is the metal cure. Especially effective for this purpose is the sound of metal.

This is why the wonderful singing bowls of Kathmandu are so precious. Made from seven different types of metal, these singing bowls, when correctly made, resonate and produce harmonics that are incredibly efficient at absorbing all "sickness chi" from the home. The use of singing bowls is something you need to practice and get used to doing. The best way to begin is to invest in a really good singing bowl. Get a small one, as the harmonics of the smaller bowls tend to be sharper and of a higher octave. Some people, however, do prefer the lower sounds of the larger bowls. It is up to you really, as both are equally efficient at dissolving sickness chi.

In my home, I purify with singing bowls made of the seven metals as well as crystal singing bowls from Germany. I find these are excellent for arresting and containing the spread of illness among the residents of a house. If you prefer to use bells, those that also are made from seven metals are best. Most powerful will be a bell with a metal striker that hits this kind of metal shell.

Cleansing with a Singing Bowl

Walk around the room three times in a clockwise direction, striking the singing bowl or rubbing its edges with a wooden mallet. This will make the bowl sing and, in singing, it creates a vibrational force that cleanses the air of sickness chi. If at first you have difficulty getting the bowl to sing, just strike it occasionally and let the sounds emitted stretch gracefully on. Keep on creating the sound of metal and, within minutes, you will feel the room grow lighter and brighter.

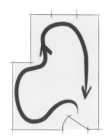

Singing bowls for healing

As you purify your house, also make sure you go through the rooms of those who are ill. Try to clear these rooms as much as you can. One of the causes of illness is sleeping in a bedroom that is infested with sickness energy emanating from clothes, surroundings, and clutter.

Use the singing bowl to purify the energy of a specific room where someone who has been very ill is convalescing. This ritual helps to ease the pain of someone who is suffering from physical ailments. It is important to do this during the period of convalescence.

What to do after losing a loved one   70

If someone has died, you must cleanse the room that the person occupied before and during the death. You may strengthen the cleansing process with the sound of a singing bowl or bowls.

When a death in the home has been caused by illness or disease, it is an excellent idea to have something that belonged to the dead person buried or cremated with the body. This symbolically buries or dissipates the disease or illness. After a Buddhist or Chinese funeral, there is usually a ritualized cleansing of the space that the dead person occupied, and generally monks are invited to perform special offerings and prayers there. My Taoist friends have explained to me that the accompanying striking of bells and the occasional clashing of cymbals during the offering ceremony is what cleanses the air and lifts the atmosphere.

It is also a good idea to simultaneously burn some incense. Choose the fragrance carefully. Use only good quality incense. The cleansing power of good incense is very intense. If in doubt, use sandalwood incense.

So gather together your tools:
* Use bells to create metal energy.
* Use incense smoke to create fire energy.

Cleanse the room previously occupied by the resident who has just passed away by going around the room three times with the bells or bowls, and then three times with incense. Chanting mantras while doing the cleansing adds to the potency of the ritual. Chanting mantras and saying prayers in accompaniment to energy-cleansing work is personal, so you must decide if you want to add this component to your ritual.

Treasures for the Afterlife

The concept of burying material possessions along with the dead person is very much a part of the Chinese tradition. This is practiced in rather an elaborate manner by wealthy families, who often place special jewelry, clothes, and books in the coffin with the corpse. In wealthier Chinese families, they often place jade in coffins—especially a jade cicada, as this aids the dead ancestor along on his journey to heaven.

These families practice this ritual even when the deceased did not die of an illness. Considering the excesses of the emperor who was buried alongside an entire terra-cotta army, thus giving China its terra-cotta soldiers, it is apparent that there is a symbolic act in letting his possessions go with him into the next world. This is something I find fascinating, especially considering the vast treasures buried alongside the Pharaohs and ministers of ancient Egypt.

71 Clearing energy after a death

Where there has just been a death in a house, it is very re-energizing to complete the "clearing of homes" ritual with sunshine water. After the ritual cleansing with bells and incense, follow it, on the seventh day, with a thorough cleansing of the house using sunshine water. Sunshine water is water that has been left out in morning sunshine for at least three hours. The Chinese like to keep urns that are filled with water outdoors so that the water is able to absorb the energy of the sun, moon, wind, air, and rain. In modern times, when we get our water from faucets, leaving it outdoors for a while is a good way for harmful chemicals like chlorine to evaporate. This softens the water considerably and makes it really excellent for a variety of purposes, one of which is to give a house a thorough cleansing.

Natural sunlight or water that has been energized by the sun helps cleanse the energy of a space after a death.

Using sunshine water
When you clean your home with sunshine water, you have to make sure that the floor is covered with water. This applies only to the ground floor of homes. Sunshine-empowered water seeps into the base of the home, revitalizing and cleansing it of any lingering death energy. If you live in an apartment, you cannot do this ritual, as it will be ineffective. In this situation, use a damp cloth soaked and rinsed with sunshine water to cleanse and revitalize the energy.

After deaths in China, symbolic cleansing is always done in this manner to help the departed soul on its way. The home the person left behind should also be infused with living yang energy to benefit the living who are still present. The Chinese and Buddhists believe that, by the seventh day after dying, the soul of the person who has passed on will have left the premises and gone on to what is known as the state of "bardo"–the state between death and rebirth. By the forty-ninth day after death, the soul will have been reborn or gone on to "Pure Land," as the heaven world is called by the Chinese.

The sacred incense cure 72

The use of incense purification rituals is very popular among Asian peoples. The idea is to create ascending spiritual smoke that connects directly to the air consciousness around us. In many Buddhist and Taoist temples, burning joss sticks of incense creates special energy for the temple environment, which is believed to purify the air around the temple. Devotees often burn joss sticks to add to the fragrance as well as to tap into the energy already created.

Always begin a purifying ritual that uses smoke and incense by first generating a quiet mind and good motivation. Open doors and windows to bring in new breezes and winds. Then follow with the sacred smoke ritual, which employs fragrant incense or aroma sticks. Many different circumstances may be improved with fragrant-smoke cleansing. This ritual is not very different from the "smudging" that Native Americans do. The main difference is the type of incense used and the direction of movement around the home. There are some traditions that encourage moving around the room in a counter-clockwise direction, as it

My Personal Incense Cure

The method I use is very "overseas Chinese" in the way it evolved in Malaysia. This is the way I was taught to do this when I was a teenager; it is the nonya method, a "Malaysianized" method. It entails using a small circular container that has a holder. I place smoldering pieces of burning charcoal on the container and, as I walk around the rooms of the house in a clockwise direction, I add fragrant, dried, herbal leaves that emit a wonderful fragrance.

I use herbs from the high mountains and, as I walk around each of the rooms, I also chant mantras under my breath. By the third circumambulation around a room, I can feel the energy there growing lighter and brighter.

Later, when I discovered other similar rites performed by Taoist and Buddhist monks, I recognized the rituals' essence as being very similar to what I had been doing, so I added the ringing of bells to my

weekly smoke ceremony. Eventually I also added the chanting of additional mantras that I learned from High Lamas.

I have since discovered that there are many wonderful variations of sacred smoke rituals that are used to cleanse the home. Some are very simple and others rather elaborate. It is up to the individual how simple or elaborate the ritual is made. All the sacred incense ingredients needed are now easily available.

is maintained that this goes back to the source. I myself always use the clockwise direction, as this symbolizes moving forward.

Setting your intent

What is most important is to focus the mind on the cleansing process and the generation of the ritual's motivation, which is to keep the energy of the living space light and bright, thereby keeping illness and misfortune at bay. Always undertake space-clearing with the motivation of making your home more auspicious and cleared of "illness chi" so that your family will benefit. This altruistic intention makes the process very powerful indeed.

73 Always use good incense for the best purification

The result of purifying your living space by burning incense is a very special kind of warmth that creates gentle embracing vibrations for the home. Everyone present becomes more tolerant, less prone to anger, and more accommodating. This is because purifying space with sacred incense really does make the energy softer, and so very nurturing.

The use of sacred smoke in rituals is something with which native groups in many countries are familiar. The actual methods, timing, and types of incense used may differ from place to place, but the general principle is the same, as is the belief that sacred aromatic smoke has the power to cleanse and purify. Tune into the kind of incense you need before

Incense is a potent purifier. It represents the cleansing energy of fire.

An Incense Ritual for Fridays

I recommend that you do this ritual every Friday around 6 in the morning or evening. This is said to be the most auspicious time to purify buildings with incense.

Walk in a clockwise direction around the edges of each room in your home with the incense smoke and watch it fill the room. Leave the windows open while doing this, so that the chi you have created will mingle with the fresh new chi flowing into the house from outdoors.

You may let the smoke waft over clothes in closets, and in storerooms, bathrooms, and toilets. Spend a little longer purifying bedrooms and studies. And always wash your hands before and after the ritual.

you begin cleansing your living space. Invest in good incense. I recommend sandalwood to begin with, since it emits a magnificent aroma that helps you transcend consciousness as you close your eyes and gentle yourself so that you can sense its vibrations. However, it is becoming increasingly difficult (and expensive) to find pure sandalwood incense, so if you are having difficulty obtaining it, do investigate what is available from India and South America. Your choice of incense is a subjective matter. Different scents affect individuals differently. If you are uncertain what to use, start with less pungent aromas; choose well-tried incenses you know before experimenting with the heavier ones from Asia.

The incense ritual requires hot, burning coal and a container. Incense used for this is usually in powder or dried leaf form. It is strewn over a hot burning medium (e.g., a piece of charcoal) so that smoke is created. Ready-made incense blocks may be used also.

Potent purifiers: herbs from the high mountains 74

Space purification using herbs picked from the high mountains are especially potent as purification agents. They give off the most heavenly fragrance and create very pure chi. I first discovered the potency of high mountain herbs when I visited Kathmandu and found Lawado incense. This incense comes from the holy Solu Khumbu region of the Himalayas, which is around 13,000 feet above sea level. Plants grow very sparsely there. Supply too is sparse. But most of the incense of this type that is sold has been mixed with other Kathmandu valley incense, so you must try to find incense from the high mountains where the air is pure and the energy contained in the herbs and leaves is also pure and powerfully invigorating.

There are also some excellent herbs known to Native Americans, who use them in their smudging and sweat lodge rituals. Sage, sweetgrass, and special pine branches provide a particularly sweet-smelling incense.

Smudge sticks are traditionally made from sage and sweetgrass.

Using natural aromas to revitalize energy 75

When you work with energy, you will discover that aromas lighten and dissolve negative and hostile energy.

It is a matter of personal preference which scents you use, although some scents have a more powerful effect than others. Sandalwood is generally acknowledged as being particularly uplifting. It is also a very spiritual scent and its wood is revered in places like China and India, where religious objects carved in sandalwood are a booming industry. When you burn sandalwood incense in your living space, you will experience the healing essence of its fragrance very quickly. Sandalwood absorbs all negative energy that is on surfaces, clothes, walls, and floors, and even in the air itself. It is wonderful to finish any kind of spring-cleaning exercise with whiffs of its fragrance by burning sandalwood incense sticks.

If you are ill, have a blocked-up nose, or have come down with the flu, lighting a stick of sandalwood incense will embrace you in an aura of healing energy that is very comforting.

Lavender is also very conducive to reducing heaviness in the air, and it is said to bring out the creative spirit of our consciousness. It is especially wonderful for those who practice meditation therapy.

Aromatherapy today blends easily with many feng shui rituals. The release of natural aromas into space through the burning of incense invokes subtle energy fields, and it is these that determine the quality of chi in any space. Fragrance and aromatic oils have tremendous healing power. Anyone can incorporate this into a powerful space-purifying ritual with great success.

76 Ways to use sound therapy to enhance chi

According to classical Chinese texts, everything in the universe takes form and shape as manifestations of two opposing yet complementary energies one being yin, the other being yang.

When energy spaces are characterized as yin, one may infer that they display the stillness of death, non-movement, and no growth. Yet within yin is always a spark of yang, which can be fanned into a roaring presence. One way to infuse yang energy into a room is through using sound. Thus, the energy of homes can come alive almost instantly. Sound therapy may utilize quite powerfully the noises of music, people, children, chimes, pets, bells and bowls, and drums and cymbals.

Every tradition uses the throbbing, rhythmic sounds of various instruments to breathe yang-life into a special day, celebration, or happy occasion. In China, it is traditional to use sounds for such times, in the form of a

Yang and Yin
Yang is movement and activity, and

Yin is stillness and non-activity.

Yang is sounds and music, while

Yin is quiet.

Yang is life and sunshine.

Yin is death and darkness.

sudden burst of firecrackers exploding during the New Year or with the beating of drums at festivals when lions are brought in to symbolically welcome yang energy. Bells and cymbals are also extensively used to awaken the chi of spaces. Thus, when wealthy people move into their homes, they go through a ritual that always includes drumbeats, bells, and cymbals clashing.

Using sound therapy at home
In your home, sound therapy may be used on a less grand scale, as home energy need not be very powerful. For this purpose, wind chimes are an excellent way of capturing natural sounds from the wind. Such chimes can be made of metal or bamboo. You can use both types–metal for the West and Northwest corners, and bamboo for the wood corners of the East and Southeast. Hang these sound-enhancers in the corners of your home but also bring in the sounds of laughter. The yang that comes from happy people is very powerful, so keep inviting your friends over to have a good time. It is far more auspicious than you realize.

Where to Place Wooden Wind Chimes

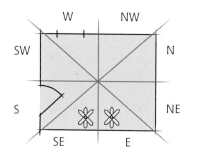

Where to Place Metal Wind Chimes

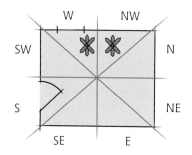

Notice that these corners face each other and lie in opposite compass directions. This is because the two elements being enhanced–here wood, which brings prosperity, and metal, which brings gold and success–are those most commonly associated with material success.

How to counter repeated accidents *77*

A six-rod metal wind chime neutralizes bad luck brought by the feng shui of time, or Flying Stars.

Negative energy in the home often causes a series of unrelated yet discernible patterns of accidents: someone hits your car, you bang your head against a ceiling beam, or fall due to a misstep. When you notice a series of little things like this happening to you, one of three things could be out of sync in your home:

Check out Flying Stars
It could be that the annual and monthly Flying Stars have brought bad luck to your front door or bedroom. It is a good idea to check this out if you can before something more serious happens. Usually the entrance of star numbers 5 and 2, either singly or together, into the part of the house where the front door is located can cause a whole month's worth of bad luck unless it is remedied by six wind chime rods. So, even if you do not know Flying Star Feng Shui, hang a small metal wind chime near the front door and note whether the accidents or illnesses stop.

An afflicted entrance
The entrance of your house could also be afflicted with excessive amounts of an element that destroys the element of the main doorway. (This kind of thing can also occur in your bedroom.) You need to know which part of the house is North and which South, and so forth, and to identify the elements of each, then you will be able to tell whether elements are in conflict. If they are, remove the offending element. For example, if you suddenly decide to place a tree in the Southwest corner of the house and your front door is located here, the chi of the front door will be sapped, so remove the tree!

A blocked entrance
Another possibility may be that the entrance is blocked by boxes or newly arrived furniture. This can cause a series of misfortunes unless rectified. No matter how busy you are, putting off clearing away newly arrived furniture or items for the house can have bad consequences.

78   What to do when relationships go wrong

If things start going wrong for you in your interactions with people, both at work and socially, you can suspect that something in the energy of your living space is having a negative effect on your relationship luck. This is usually caused by afflicted earth energy in the home, which in turn can be caused by the simple passage of time (the cause for which could be the entry of bad Flying Stars into your bedroom or around your front door), or by the placement of plants in the wrong part of the home. Plants signify wood energy and when these are inadvertently placed in earth corners (Southwest and Northeast), they cause problems in your social interactions with people.

Junk and sensitive corners

Sometimes, in clearing the clutter of your home, you could unwittingly have placed junk inside what I call halfway-house boxes. These then get placed inside spare rooms, bedrooms, or perhaps in corners, just left there pending your arrangement for them to be carted away. If your luck is bad, these can trigger negative effects simply because the

If your relationships are unhappy, check out the Southwest and Northeast sectors of your home.

newly created boxes of junk and garbage have been dumped in wrong corners that cause feng shui afflictions to manifest. The most vulnerable areas are main doorways and bedrooms. When things suddenly start going wrong, check that the flow of chi is not blocked and that plants have not been placed in the wrong corners.

If all seems well here, the cause could be your Flying Stars, in which case hang a small metal wind chime near the door and watch whether things get better. If they do, you are on the right track and hanging another wind chime will strengthen the remedy. If things grow worse, then it is a really good idea to arrange for a Flying Star natal chart of the house to be done. This will immediately give you a map of the luck of the house and show you what has gone wrong.

Removing Plants for Happiness

To strengthen relationships, boost the earth element and remove all plants in the Northeast and Southwest sectors of your home and individual rooms.

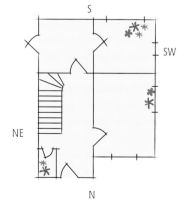

How to defuse confrontation 79

Quarrels and arguments are another way that afflicted feng shui can manifest. When a husband and wife start quarreling for no apparent or logical reason, the culprit is usually an afflicted bedroom. In Flying Star Feng Shui, there is a quarrelsome star number that "flies" into bedrooms; it flies into different areas of the home both annually and monthly. The Chinese use the Chinese Almanac to calculate such feng shui afflictions and remedy these quarrelsome stars. Usually the most effective remedy for them is to place something red and gold in the bedroom.

I have discovered that when my family is going through a period when everyone is being argumentative, quarrelsome, hostile, and confrontational, it is almost always due to the quarrelsome star having flown into the dining or family room. For this reason, I have placed something red and gold in both the dining and family room.

Cures for this can take the form of paintings or specially made auspicious objects. If you do not know how to check for the presence of this quarrelsome star, just use the cure suggested when you discern a sudden rise in family tensions. It will go a long way towards easing tensions. You should also reduce the amount of noise in rooms where the family gathers, as noise triggers the hostility star in the Flying Star natal chart.

Using crystals to dissolve tension 80

Another really excellent way of dissolving tension within the home is by the placement of six round crystal balls in the family areas of the home, especially in the Southwest or Northwest corners. Six crystal balls are said to encourage a smoothness in relationships, while the number 6 signifies heaven. The crystal balls symbolize a union of the heaven trigram with the earth trigram i.e., Chien with Kun. Crystals are the most potent symbols of earth energy, not to mention wonderful enhancers and very auspicious. But do make sure you buy crystals, not plastic that passes as crystal. Also, natural crystals are superior to man-made crystals.

An excellent energy enhancer is to shine a light on a large single-pointed natural crystal in or near the center of your home. The light activates the power of the crystal's earth energy and, since the center of the home is always enhanced by the earth element, everyone living in the home will benefit. Tension within the home will start to dissolve and any tendency towards anger, violence, and hostility will be considerably reduced.

Crystal Cleansing

Here is a preliminary cleansing ritual to perform when you bring a crystal into your home. Always cleanse it of other people's energy by first placing it in a salt solution. Use either sea salt or rock salt. Or rub salt all over the surface of the crystal. Imagine that the salt is drawing out all the negative energy, then wipe the stone with a damp cloth. If the crystal is very large, you may want to soak it in the salt solution for seven days and seven nights. Once a crystal has been cleansed, the continuous shining of a light onto it will keep its chi fresh and vibrant.

81 The yin water cure to banish anger

When continuous anger leads to violence and loud quarreling among family members in a home, it is a very good idea to invest in a vase to apply the Yin Water Cure. The Chinese word for vase is ping, which stands for peace; often Chinese homes display many beautiful vases to create an atmosphere of peace and harmony there. Vases, however, work their potent magic only when filled with water and displayed in homes that are clear of clutter. The water is Yin Water, which has the power to absorb and dilute anger.

If the quarrels and anger are between lovers and spouses, the water can be made more powerful if it is moon-empowered Yin Water. Place an urn full of water in the grounds of your home or on the balcony of your apartment on the night of the full moon. Let the water absorb the energy of the moon and

then bring the water inside your home. Poured into beautiful vases, they act as powerful keepers of the peace.

Sometimes hanging a painting of a scene with a vase in the moonlight also simulates this cure. Taoist feng shui masters are very clever at using paintings to create special kinds of chi vibrations inside homes, and I have spent many happy hours fascinated by the stories they have told me.

Once a Taoist feng shui master visited our office and, spying a painting of running horses, he stopped and said, "Look at the faces of these horses: they are white with fear. Such a painting suggests panic. It cannot be auspicious." And, indeed, he was right. It was a very small painting done by an insignificant artist, which I had over-looked. I took it down immediately.

Overcoming lethargy with bells 82

If your home suffers from lethargic energy, its residents will feel similarly lethargic. An air of tediousness and monotony hangs in such a home, which can be very debilitating. If you are feeling this way, chances are the chi of your home is tired. Its carpets, curtains, and walls have become exhausted through nothing more than the passage of time.

The home's chi needs revitalizing, and renovating it will help. Renovations, however simple, always move the chi and are good for a house's residents, as it immediately revitalizes the place. But renovations cost money and not everyone can afford them on a regular basis.

In such cases, I recommend the use of sound to wake up the chi. Bells are very efficient for this. They do not cleanse the space, but they move energy within it, and the result is a massive infusion into the house of yang chi. Use metal bells, as the sound of metal permeates the earth and moves through walls.

In this context, the sound of metal upon metal is better than wood on metal. Invest in a special bell that is made from seven types of metals—including gold and silver, which symbolizes the sun and moon. These bells emit a much longer-lasting harmonic. Moreover, they signify the seven planets of our solar system as well as the seven chakra points of the human body. The seven-metal bell is a very efficient tool for improving the energy in space. Try it the next time that you feel down in the dumps.

Ringing a space-clearing bell wakes up lethargic chi energy and revitalizes the atmosphere.

Clearing legal entanglement chi 83

Legal problems are usually the result of entanglement stars in the Flying Star natal chart becoming activated. A feng shui practitioner can be very specific when diagnosing areas that may be afflicted, which enables residents to install remedies in the home. According to Flying Star Feng Shui, legal problems are caused by the hostile entanglement number 3 afflicting the relationship star in the house's natal chart; this can recur annually.

For those who do not understand the Flying Star method of diagnosis, you can install the cure of moon-energized water by putting yin water in a vase. You can also give your home a thorough cleansing with moon-energized water that has been standing still for at least three days and nights.

Yin water helps absorb the quarrelsome vibrations that lead to legal entanglements. Remove all wind chimes, clocks, and other moving objects from the vicinity of the front door. Place an image or a figurine of a bird in flight there, flying outward, to reduce the negative impact of legal battles; it may even solve the problem altogether. Birds are usually excellent symbols of appeasement and they also ward off accidents. Keeping bird feathers or the image of a bird in a car is also said to have the same effect.

84 What to do after a burglary

Houses that have just suffered the nasty aftershock of being robbed, burgled, and broken into need to be instantly cleansed of the negative energy. You will find that usually it is the same few houses in a neighborhood that tend to be the targets of burglars. The Chinese believe that such houses suffer from the Robbery Affliction Star and, unless this is corrected, the danger of being burgled is always present. Residents from such homes also tend to be more prone to petty robbery.

The cause can be due to the intangible energy of bad Flying Stars, or it can also be caused by the way rooms within the home are laid out. Finding the cause of a propensity to burglary using compass charts is a very powerful dimension of feng shui practice, but it is time-consuming. An easier method is to cleanse the energy as an immediate measure of protection and then to install cures that protect from similar misfortunes striking again in the future.

Cleansing with salt and saffron

Saffron is used to cleanse and purify buildings in the East.

When your house has just been burgled, use a mixture of salt and saffron water to cleanse the doorways and windows of the home. All the openings of the home should get a wipe with this solution. Move three times around the openings in a clockwise direction.

Next, place this solution by the doorway for three days, and keep the lights turned on there for at least three days too.

You can also use the singing bowl to absorb any left-over negative energy. Usually when a home has been burgled, residents live in fear during the weeks afterwards. It is very necessary to lift this cloud of apprehension; otherwise, negative energy is created that can act as the catalyst for some other type of misfortune to occur. Using the comforting harmonics of a singing bowl to absorb the negative energy is really very helpful. The internal chi of residents will become stabilized in a shorter time and the air lighter.

The broom trick

An effective antidote to being burgled is to place an inverted broom beside the wall next to a door leading outside. This is said to ward off the chi of robbery. The Chinese also believe that placing a pair of Chinese unicorns (Chi Lins) or lions flanking the doorway acts as a powerful deterrent.

The Power of Chi Lins

The Chi Lin, or Chinese unicorn, is a celestial protector. If you live in a bungalow, place a pair of stone Chi Lins high above the gates on your property to act as guardians.

If you live in an apartment or flat, place a pair outside the door to your personal apartment. Use powerful glue to stick the lions onto the floor if you need to (provided too that this does not break any residency rules!) Always place the Chi Lins so they face outward, and symbolically confront any threat or negativity that tries to enter the home.

Revitalizing energy after a tragedy 85

In the aftermath of the September 11th bombing in 2001, I recall moving through my home in a kind of stupor. I had watched the whole horrific scene on television and for days thereafter the images stayed in my mind, refusing to go away. That was when I realized how it must feel when one experiences tragedy and how much worse it is when the tragedy touches us in a personal way, and affects our home–the place we think of as our sanctuary.

Tragedy strikes in many ways. Sometimes it is brought on by natural calamities e.g., fire, earthquake, thunderstorms, typhoons, floods. These are big tragedies caused by imbalances in the chi of the larger environment, and Man usually cannot do much about them. When the earth dragons roar, they bring about earthquakes, volcanic eruptions, and forest fires, causing death and destruction. When the sea dragons are displeased, they whip up the winds, causing waters to rise and winds to blow strong. These bring the terror of water energy in its most destructive form.

Chinese beliefs

The Chinese believe that, in the wake of such natural disasters, the land becomes cleansed, as all negative things are swept away in the most powerful manner of purification. They believe that all that is left to do is to rebuild. Against the onslaughts of nature, man is quite helpless.

But when tragedy is man-made, the energy left behind remains ugly and dangerous. In feng shui, there are three types of bad chi. There is negative chi, dead chi, and killing chi. All three are dangerous, but the most

harmful is killing chi. The aftermath of tragedy leaves behind dead chi and, unless this is swept away or reawakened in some way, it causes a buildup of yin energy.

The antidote to dead chi is a massive infusion of yang energy, which can take the form of sounds, activity, and lights. These are three sources of yang energy that can be used to bring energy to life.

If your home has suffered flooding, or been destroyed by fire, the sheer act of rebuilding it brings back yang energy. When tragedy comes in the form of accidents or death to residents, then the dead chi in the home must be rekindled with bright lights and happy sounds.

Creating a personal altar of bright lights brings help and healing in the aftermath of a tragedy. This is also practiced in organized religion in Western churches and cathedrals, and in many Eastern temples.

86　How to dissolve gossip

If you suffer from gossip at work or in your social life, the best way to reduce its occurrence and effect on you is to use sounds to scare away the devil of chatter. Metal cymbals are best for this purpose. Hanging a pair of cymbals just inside the home will symbolically override the negative effects of gossip and go a long way towards reducing its occurrence as well.

Another very effective way to reduce gossip in your life is by utilizing crystal energy. For this, display six very smooth crystal balls, made of white crystal or in a variety of light shades–pink to calm the chatter that focuses on your love life, green to put a stop to idle talk that pertains to your business, blue to counter conversation that harms your career, and lilac to reduce all frivolous gossip.

These light-colored crystal balls do not just absorb all the negative energies associated with bad mouthing and politicking; they also create harmony and success for the inhabitants of the home in which they are located.

Crystal balls indicate life that is smooth, without aggravation and rancor. In my own home, I place six crystal balls in my living room as well as my home office. They ensure that my work and all my projects move forward smoothly, with little or no aggravation. All negative energy is absorbed by them.

In order to use crystal balls this way, place them quite low–a coffee table is an ideal place for them, since this sets them in the center of the room. They do not need to be very large (three-inch [8.5 cm] diameter balls are about right) or of any particular color. Many people prefer them to be clear crystal, but recently beautiful crystal balls in different colors have become available, and prompted me to bring more color into my feng shui cures; I must say that they have helped to create a smoother and much nicer lifestyle for me.

The best area in which to place crystal balls, for overcoming idle gossip and frivolous chatter, is the Southwest–the place of the Matriarch. This can refer to the Southwest of the whole house or the Southwest of the living room. Wipe the crystal balls daily to keep them clear and clean. When they become blurred due to a buildup of grime and dust, they tend to lose their potency.

Placing Crystals

Placing crystal balls in the Southwest of the home banishes gossip and promotes harmony.

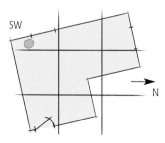

Displaying crystal balls symbolically strengthens the Matriarch, who resides in the Southwest corner.

When you are the victim of politicking 87

If you are a victim of politicking at work, it is imperative to do something about it. The Taoist feng shui cure for harmful gossip is the rooster image. It is believed to be the most effective countermeasure for those who inadvertently become victims of harmful and malicious politicking at work. Place a white rooster on your table or desk at the office and let it peck away all of your problems one by one. The rooster cure is especially suitable for those whose desks are placed in tight corners or who are sitting in what I like to refer to as the centipede arrangement: one desk behind another in two rows. Such an arrangement gives rise to the sting of gossip and malicious backbiting. The rooster on your desk will clear away all negative energy created by this situation.

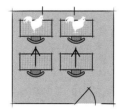 

If you have to sit with others behind you (left) or in a tight corner (right) place the rooster on your desk to protect yourself from gossip.

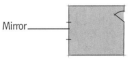

Mirror

Place a brass mirror in your foyer or hall to prevent gossip following you home.

Getting help from mirrors

To ensure that you are adequately protected, also place a brass mirror in your home–in a corner diagonal to the main door. The brass mirror cure was a popular method used by the mandarins of the Chinese Emperor's court to overcome any negative effect of political intrigues. In those days, the danger of death caused by the maneuvering of ministers and court advisers was very real. Any fall from grace would result in imprisonment or death not only of the patriarch but also his entire family. Belief in symbolic feng shui was something everyone took for granted, especially the advisers in the Emperor's court.

Today's corporate and office intrigues are not actually dissimilar from the Court intrigues of those days, so feng shui cures used in those times may provide some relief. Brass and other kinds of auspicious mirrors were used to counter negative politicking. Mirrors made of glass, metal, or any reflective surface are believed to reflect back any negativity that people send your way. Various methods are used to empower these mirrors; popular is reflecting the energy of the sun from a glass mirror to transform others' negative intentions towards you into positive ones.

Protecting your home from gossip

Meanwhile, brass mirrors strategically placed facing the main door from a corner are said to be able to deflect all negative energy that enters the home, especially negative energy caused by politicking and competitive pressures. If you have an altar in your home (as most Chinese have), place the brass mirror on its tabletop and let it reflect as much of the room and the entrance area as possible. This has the effect of deflecting all bad intentions attempting to enter through the doorway.

88 Special amulets and space-clearing to dispel powerful envy

You could be the unwitting recipient of powerful negative vibrations sent your way by jealous colleagues, spurned lovers, envious friends, or business enemies. In today's highly competitive world, everyone needs protection against the envy and jealousy of unscrupulous people.

Many Asians wear amulets and talismans that are said to have the power to ward off negative energy. The Chinese are also great believers in amulets, and many think that simply wearing a dragon pin has the power to ward off negative vibrations. Other popular amulets are horses, Chi Lins, and mystic symbols.

Wear the dragon pin to protect yourself from others' envy.

In a later section of this book, I have presented some excellent techniques that you can use in order to empower symbols of protection. These techniques were passed on to me by very high spiritual and Taoist practitioners during the course of my corporate career. I share these empowerments with you here because they are for protection, and have no power at all to harm anyone. These techniques are excellent for warding off negative arrows–from hostility to general bad feeling–that may be sent your way.

What to do if others are jealous

If you feel that you could be attracting jealousy, wear a dragon pin. This is a very simple amulet, used for many centuries. As a powerful celestial creature, the dragon helps protect you from negative influences, and also attracts good luck.

A woman should wear a dragon pin on her left, while a man should wear a dragon pin on his right. The pin is necessary because symbolically it represents a needle capable of piercing through negative chi. In the old days, Taoist masters would sew needles into the clothing of children to ward off jealousy and envy.

Fending off bad intentions

Once a week, it also is an excellent idea to perform a space-clearing ritual in your home using a singing bowl (see Tips 69, 114). This regular ritual will continue to absorb any lingering negative energies brought home by its working residents. When you make this a regular ritual, supplemented with incense cures, anyone with bad intentions towards you will find it very difficult to enter your home.

Swords to Banish Jealousy

A talisman very effective at clearing negative intangibles that may affect the well-being of inhabitants are the metal curved knife and the "coin sword," which is made of old Chinese coins tied together with red thread. They are said to slice through invisible negative energy with great accuracy and effectiveness. Place them behind you at work to curb the negative impact of jealous thoughts sent your way by envious colleagues.

CHAPTER FOUR

CLEARING NEGATIVE CHI THAT AFFECTS YOUR RELATIONSHIPS

The negative energy of a broken relationship 89

Bad feng shui is one of the most common causes of broken relationships and marriages. When the energy of the home turns bad, or quarrelsome stars fly into the bedroom (as part of "evolution of time dimension" feng shui), problems start to disturb the relationships of spouses, other members of their family, and outsiders. The chi that has a negative effect on marriages is the most harmful of these.

A mirror opposite the bed, a "poison arrow" affliction from the table to the left of the bed (see above) and general junk and laundry in the corner afflict the energy of this bedroom. This creates negativity in the relationship of the couple sleeping here.

Quarrels and misunderstandings are manifestations of disharmony in the environment. These are caused as much by spatial energy working against the relationship as by the negative intangible energy brought by bad Flying Star numbers into bedrooms. Over the past thirty years of observing relationship breakups, I have discovered that a large number of broken marriages occur in homes where the bedroom has a feng shui affliction.

When you know about relationship luck and feng shui, you know there are taboos specific to bedrooms, which, if broken, cause strains to develop between the partners inhabiting it.

Of course other afflictions can create similar strains in a relationship, including bad Flying Star energy. It is useful to know enough about feng shui so you can ensure that the spatial energy of your bedroom is conducive to a loving relationship.

If you are the spouse left behind in the marital home, thoroughly cleanse your house to clear the negative chi remaining there from angry words, unhappiness, and grief. Using sound therapy will break through the pall of gloom that hangs over your home. Play happy music and use a singing bowl to capture and transform negative chi into positive chi. Remove any afflictions you can find. For instance, change all the sheets and curtains in the bedroom to get rid of old bad energy. Thoroughly remodeling your bedroom, alone, will make you feel very energized. Clearing all the negative energy that a broken marital union leaves behind in a home will help to create new energy, which will give you strength to move forward.

Three Ways to Avoid a Split

1. Mirrors in a couple's bedroom cause an outside third party to disrupt their relationship, and put severe strain upon it, causing infidelity. A mirror directly facing the marital bed is the most dangerous cause of this affliction.

2. Having water inside a bedroom in a fish tank or fountain, or even a painting showing water–especially hung just above the bed–will cause loss for both parties in the marriage. Water in the bedroom is a major taboo in feng shui.

3. Two separate mattresses on a couple's double-bed frame will create an invisible split in their relationship, which will manifest during an astrological time that is bad for them.

90 Clearing negative energy from your sleeping space

It is your sleeping space that either benefits or harms you most. Once I went through a period when I woke up every morning filled with a sense of dread. My back would ache terribly and my mouth would be dry and have a bitter taste. At first I thought I was coming down with something, but I observed that, as each day progressed, I would feel better.

An amethyst geode placed under the foot of the bed strengthens a couples' relationship.

This made me suspect that something was wrong with my sleeping space. On the wall behind my bed I discovered that a small ledge had somehow fallen down, leaving behind six exposed nails. There they were, sticking out and pointing straight at my head as I slept. Without further ado, I had them removed.

Then I gave my mattress and pillows a sunshine bath to dissolve any left-over negative energies that might be clinging to the pillows. I placed them in the hot sunshine for three days in a row. The result was simply amazing. For the first time in months, I slept soundly and woke up feeling refreshed and well rested.

Tips for women

Your sleeping space must always be checked for and cleared of negative energy. When a couple break up, the sleeping space should be cleared immediately. If you are the wife and your husband leaves you, you should give your mattress and pillows a sunshine bath to infuse them with yang

energy. Then place an amethyst geode under your bed, just where your feet usually rest on the mattress.

Tips for men

If you are a man and your partner has just left you, or you have just discovered that she is having an affair and you want her back, place an amethyst geode under your feet. This is believed to strengthen the bond between mother and father, as is the practice of husbands sleeping on the left and wives on the right-hand side of the bed. Do not, however, place the amethyst crystal directly under your head, as this will disturb your sleep; its energy is too powerful. The placement of crystal below your feet is a powerful Taoist method of ensuring that couples stay together happily.

Three Cures for Negativity

1. If you place an amethyst geode under your bed, you also need to cleanse it regularly (see Tip 104).
2. For extra bedroom purification, expose your mattress and pillows to bright sunshine.
3. At least once a month, light fragrant incense and walk around your bed clockwise, three times. This removes any lingering negativity around your sleeping space.

Clutter-clearing and cleansing of the bed space   91

I encourage all couples to undertake regular, systematic space cleansing of their bed. Start by clearing out all the clutter under the bed. It is vital to throw out the junk, no matter how sentimental you may be about the things kept there.

In the old days, when banks did not exist, many families literally slept with the family gold under the bed in the belief that this would safeguard their assets. A symbolic bowl of coins is therefore considered auspicious, as are crystals–often referred to as the treasures of the earth–under a bed. However, be cautious about which treasures are suitable to be stored here. Never place old clothes, books, albums, files, or personal memorabilia under a bed. Those with genuine value should be placed inside a gold box in a higher place. The symbolism of sleeping above personal items that are closely associated with you will press down your good luck. Photographs of your children placed under your bed will hinder their growth and development. Sleeping over photographs of the family breadwinner will similarly press down on their luck.

Keeping the underbed area clutter free safeguards you from sleeping over photographs or items that you associate with important family members, which symbolically presses down on their luck and afflicts the family.

Activating good fortune

It is also useful to regularly do a cleansing ritual of the bed space with incense and a singing bowl once a month. This will activate good fortune for your family. When the energy of the marital bed is systematically cleansed of negative energy, the chi does not have a chance to grow stale or die. This ensures that "family luck" remains vibrant and energized.

At the same time, it is important to get rid of all killing energy caused by secret poison arrows. These emanate from the sharp edges of walls and furniture and also from harmful heavy structural beams. Killing energy, or shar chi, poses immediate threats to a home's residents. Negative energy is also harmful, but its effect is less pointed and experienced over a longer period of time. Although both should be cleared, killing energy intensifies any danger to relationships, especially those of couples.

When the bed is afflicted by killing energy, there is no goodwill possible between the couple sharing it, and all their interactions will move their relationship progressively downhill. There definitely will be no descendants' luck. Even if they already have children, their family will not feel like a unit. Personally, I feel that the absence of good family luck is the saddest of all feng shui afflictions.

92 Purification procedures for your sleeping area

Saffron is a traditional purifier used ritually in Eastern cultures.

Prepare a jug of purifying saffron water to cleanse the space your bed occupies. It should be placed in a container specially designated for this purpose. After saffron has been soaked in warm water for a while, it turns the water yellow. Use the best quality saffron you can find–a few strands in a jug of warm water is all you will need. Also prepare some fragrant herbal incense for this, either in powder or block incense form. Saffron water and incense are really excellent for cleansing the bedroom, especially the area around the marriage bed.

Saffron is a very powerful substance for purifying space. It is used in many Taoist cleansing rituals, and features prominently in Hindu and Taoist puja ceremonies as well. In these rituals, saffron water is used to symbolically cleanse the body, mind, and speech of devotees participating in the puja. Saffron is considered one of the most potent of purifying agents (the best form of it comes from Greece).

Also, it complements the feng shui arrangements already in your bedroom, and has the power to cure all afflictions caused by the monthly and annual Flying Stars that affect it. So you should be able to use it with confidence. The best thing about incense and saffron cleansing is that, while it diffuses negative chi, it does no harm to anything positive or auspicious.

The Saffron Ritual

This saffron and incense cleansing ritual can be done once a month. It takes only five minutes and is very powerful.

First, walk three times around the bed in a clockwise direction, allowing the smoke from the incense to waft over it. Next, create an invisible cocoon of protection around it by sprinkling the saffron water as you walk around it three more times.

A powerful mirror ritual for reconciliations 93

Two types of separations occur when couples split up: temporary and karmic. If a separation is karmic, nothing you do will bring back the loved one, because your karma with each other has ended. The Chinese (both Taoists and Buddhists) accept that we are all "fated to be with the ones we end up starting a family with" and that our destinies with each other are based exclusively on our "heaven luck." But the Chinese also recognize that heaven luck can be speeded up or delayed, and that it makes up only a third of our destiny. There is also "earth luck" that we can harness (feng shui) and our own "mankind luck," which we can use to influence, modify, speed up, or slow down our heaven luck. So we can do something to influence our own destiny; it is not carved in stone.

Many Chinese stories tell of powerful cures and antidotes that were freely used in the Emperors' courts, especially by competing concubines desperate for the Emperor's favor. One such ritual, said to be all-power-

ful in drawing a loved one back was related to me one evening by a feng shui master. I have never tried it myself, having no reason to do so, but a couple of my girlfriends (alas, with philandering husbands) have, and they swear by it. I suspect that its level of success depends on the strength of the relaxed motivation that must accompany the performance of the ritual, as well as the severity of the split between you.

For the mirror spell, you will need two mirrors or one that is hinged and will bend backwards in which you enclose your photographs.

The Mirror Spell

First, you need a photograph of the person who has left you. A head-and-shoulders picture will be fine, but a full-bodied picture is more powerful. Do make certain that there is no one else in the picture, which should have been taken of that person alone. Cropped pictures cannot be used. Pictures taken outdoors are more potent than pictures taken indoors. It is also to be preferred if the person is smiling and happy. Photographs of the person standing are preferable to sitting or lying down poses.

- Take a corresponding photograph of yourself, alone and smiling. If you use a half-body picture of your loved one, you should use something similar of yourself.

- Now take two pieces of mirror that are the same size as the pictures. Place the two pictures so that they face each other.

- Then place the mirrors outside the joined pictures. They should reflect outwards. What you will have are two pictures (of you and your loved one) sandwiched between two mirrors. Use strong tape to tape the mirrors together with the pictures inside.

- At the time of the next full moon, catch the reflection of the moon on the surfaces of both mirrors. This washes the pictures with moon glow, said to call forth the magic of the God of marriage residing in the moon. Keep the pictures sandwiched between the mirrors until your loved one calls you and arranges to meet you. As soon as this happens, release the pictures.

The rest is up to you. This ritual does not control anyone–it simply creates an opportunity for you both to iron out your differences.

94 Calling back a loved one

Sometimes the separation between a couple is due to bad feng shui, which causes a third party to come between them. This is usually the most common situation for breakups, which is why I am a strong advocate of gaining some feng shui knowledge. Prevention is always better than cure. If you know about the taboos that can lead to infidelity, and you prevent the presence of these features in your shared home, you will be able to guard against them.

Birds are very auspicious and feature regularly in many Taoist rituals. They are said to represent safety and security. They also bring opportunities into the home, and, if you wish to sell your house, you can also use the bird ritual to do so.

Bird motifs are auspicious for the home. Displaying a bird flying toward a home symbolically calls back a loved one.

How to Protect Your Relationship

1. Never have a body of water (e.g., a pond, pool, or an aquarium) to the left of a bedroom door–that is, the left when looking from the inside facing out. Water here, no matter how auspicious according to other feng shui formulas or systems, will make the man in the relationship develop a roving eye.

2. Never have water inside your home directly facing the front door. A water feature set straight in front of an entrance to a house will cause the husband living there to develop a love interest outside his marriage. Do be careful a water feature does not conform to this taboo.

3. Never have mirrors reflecting the marriage bed. The reflection of the marriage bed in a mirror almost always brings separation. Television sets and computer screens are also said to act as mirrors. If you have a TV in your bedroom, always cover up the screen while you sleep. If you have mirrors facing the bed, either cover them or have them removed all together. This is a taboo that can make either the husband or the wife walk out of the marriage.

4. If your spouse has already left and you want to entice him/her home, put an image of a flying bird (facing outward) on the left side of the front door and place his picture next to the bird. The bird should appear to be flying inward, not outward. Shine a bright light at the bird and the loved one's picture to activate this symbolic ritual of calling back the loved one. You can use a drawing of a bird or a photograph, but the bird should be flying into the home.

Making the rift permanent and complete 95

Energy sticks to material things so, when a couple separate for good, I usually recommend moving to a new home; however, if you are staying on in the same house, then clear out all your ex-partner's belongings and personal possessions: clothes, books, files, and photographs all hold potent reminders of the old marriage. It is best to cleanse the home of this past energy if you want a chance to start afresh.

Select a day with bright sunshine and a mild breeze. Make use of wind energy to blow away the old chi–open all the doors and windows and imagine the wind clearing and refreshing your living space. Next, sprinkle sea salt around your home. Sense what kind of energy is present after you have done these simple space-clearing exercises. If, afterwards, you feel that the energy of the person lingers, the following is a ritual that is both extremely powerful and very auspicious for the well-being of your former spouse.

The boat ritual
Make a paper boat that can float on water. Inside, place the name of your former spouse with a well-meaning and well-intentioned good-bye wish. Make sure your wish is genuine. Place five offerings inside the boat–flowers, an incense stick, a coin, and a sprinkling of saffron water. These represent the five elements and show that you wish him or her well in their new life. However, do not place their picture inside the boat; just take it to a river and let it drift downriver. Do not look back once you have set the boat adrift. This will close one chapter of your life, allowing the next to unfold.

For a permanent rift, cast the boat spell using saffron, earth, incense, flowers, and a coin.

Moon-activated water 96

Moon-activated water brings loving energy into all of your living spaces. Place a large urn of water in sight of the full moon to obtain moon-activated water. Choose a night that is clear, bright, and beautiful. If there is rain or the moon is hidden behind clouds, its energy will be weak. Bright moonlight energy is what is needed. Exposure to the moonlight for one evening is sufficient to activate the water.

Use it immediately the next day either to cleanse your house or, better yet, to mix with your bath water. Add seven types of flowers that include the five elements' colors. For example: a yellow chrysanthemum for the earth element; a white lily for metal; an iris for water; a red rose for fire; and a pale green dahlia for wood, plus two other blooms to make up the seven. This is a wonderfully invigorating bathing ritual which has, in recent years, become very popular in health spas.

The Balinese are especially good at creating moon-energized flower baths. They add drops of scent to this water to make the baths more romantic. Many of the tropical plants used in health spas in Bali also have invigorating properties.

You can create similar purifying rituals in your own home. Using moon-energized water in your baths will add "loving chi" to them.

97 Balancing the yin and yang of space

Sometimes the illness and misfortune that befall a home's inhabitants are due to unbalanced air that is caused by excessive dryness. When air is especially dry or polluted, the pervading chi of a living space becomes weak and overly yang. Spraying the air with water droplets is an excellent way for restoring balance in this situation.

The yin and yang balance of air in the home exerts tremendous influence on the prevailing mood of the household. It actually influences how residents feel. Scientists measuring air pollution have been astounded by the immense difference that polluted air makes to people's moods when they are exposed to it.

This is because, of all the examples of yin/yang imbalance in the atmosphere, probably the most serious is the imbalance that is caused by polluted air. Sometimes being exposed to certain yin energy-bearing winds can cause this imbalance. Examples of such winds are the Mistral winds of Europe, the Chinook winds of North America, and the typhoons that hit some of the countries bordering the South China Sea and the Pacific Ocean. When air is unbalanced, those who breathe it may suffer from migraines, tiredness, and fatigue. This is because, when air is

Moistening the air by misting with water may help improve air quality and temperatures. Lavender (shown below) in its essential oil form can be added to the water to create a relaxing ambience.

unbalanced, the body reacts negatively; it also has a negative effect on the way people act and interact with each other.

"Balancing" the air for better health

If you notice that members of your family tend to be irritable and short-tempered, succumbing frequently to allergies, headaches, and feeling depressed for no reason, you have every reason to suspect an imbalance in the air. Spray water into the air to soften it, thereby repairing this imbalance. Or turn on a fan to increase the flow of chi. Even if you do not feel the air is polluted or dirty, spray some water droplets into it. You will be surprised at how effective this can be in improving the tempers and attitudes of those in the home. This is because water also has a very calming effect. If you wish, you can add a few drops of lavender to it, or another scent that soothes you.

Five-element therapy for great relationships   98

Anyone can use five-element therapy, which is based on the cycles of the five elements, to improve relationships. These five elements are water, wood, fire, earth, and metal. The Chinese believe that everything in the world–from compass directions to shapes, colors, days, hours, objects, and so forth–belong to one of these elements. Also, each of the eight main directions of the compass symbolizes good or bad luck associated with each member of the family, or each person in your life.

To improve your relationship with a loved one, activate the Southwest of your bedroom. If you live alone, also focus on this area because it represents romance, marriage, and family happiness. However, it also signifies your mother, older aunts, and grandmother, so activating it also benefits

Boosting the Southwest area of your home supports the role of the Matriarch.

your relationships with them. The element of the Southwest is earth, so this corner benefits from the presence of beautiful natural crystals, mountain energy, and light energy. This is because light (fire) produces earth.

Boosting relationships with bosses

To improve your relationship with your boss, employer, father, or anyone who is superior to you at work or in your social activities, activate the Northwest–this corner governs the luck of your relationships with these people. If you are in politics, this corner will also enhance your standing with your supporters. Place six metal wind chimes, or a simulated metal mountain of gold or diamonds, here. There are many ways to simulate this in your home, from displaying art and gold-leafed bolders to raw crystals strewn with cut crystals that look like diamonds.

The Directions for Harmony

If you wish to improve your relationships with colleagues, siblings, and friends, here are some guidelines to follow:

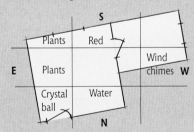

1. With males older than you, activate the East with plants, trees, and flowers.

2. With males the same age as you, activate the North with water.

3. With males younger than you, activate the Northeast with a crystal ball.

4. With females older than you, place plants in the Southeast.

5. With females the same age as you, put anything red in the South.

6. With females younger than you, put small metal wind chimes in the West.

99 Energizing the Southwest with yellow

Of all the eight corners of the home, the most important one that affects your relationship luck as a whole is the Southwest. This is the corner and wall of your home that definitely should not be too cluttered. When energy here becomes confused or afflicted, it affects all of your relationships, so it is worthwhile to invest time and effort looking after your Southwest rooms. Keep the area free of unwanted junk and, once a week, spend a few moments clearing away whatever has built up here. Do not place plants in the Southwest, as this kills the energy of earth. And never place wind chimes here, because metal depletes the Southwest of energy. The only time that metal wind chimes should be hung here is when the Flying Star affliction flies into the Southwest, which will next happen in 2010. This is because the cycles of time occur in nines to reflect the nine numbers used in Flying Star feng shui.

A yellow feature wall stimulates the energy of the Matriarch in a household.

Boosting your social life

Your social life and love life will benefit from an energy boost in the Southwest. One sure way to jumpstart a lagging social life is to paint the Southwest wall a bright sunshine yellow. This not only simulates the energy of earth, but it also adds a dose of precious yang chi here. Yellow is a particularly good color for the Southwest, the Northeast, the West, and the Northwest–but it works wonderful magic for all of your relationships in the Southwest.

However, be cautious about going overboard with this. You can have too much of this or any color in a house, so use it as a feature color. If you do not want it on your walls, you can have it as curtains, cushion covers, or carpets. To activate it further, you can shine a bright light on the color to emphasize earth energy.

In many Asian cultures, yellow was an imperial color. In old China, for instance, only the Emperors and their families were allowed to wear yellow. Here in Malaysia, yellow is also a royal color, and only members of royal families can wear it to official state dinners and garden parties.

Washing the Southwest with bright lights   100

The Southwest corner can also be washed and empowered with bright lights. This is because fire energy produces earth energy–and the placement of bright lights here lifts up any tired chi, revitalizing it instantly. When any of your relationships are flagging, or you yourself seem to be feeling tired or exhausted, you can use fire energy in the Southwest to give you a boost.

Southwest rooms with poor lighting will have their energy depleted. You simply must add fresh new lighting. When I redecorated my Southwest office at home, we were coming into the year 2001, when the Southwest was affected by the Five-Yellow affliction, which brings illness and loss. So I could not use the room that year. To lower the strength of the lights in that room, I fitted it with very weak, dim lighting.

In 2002, when the South-west became, once again, auspicious for relationships, and for me (because of my Kua number, the Southwest is especially auspicious for me), I changed the lights immediately to give the office a boost. The change was instant. My creativity returned. I cannot tell you how much easier

it is to work in that room now. I plan to install crystal lights to further enhance my productivity in this Southwest room; you can do the same. Note that any room in your home that is located in the Northeast or South also benefits from bright lights.

Candles in crystal holders create earth and fire energy, which boosts Southwest rooms and corners.

101 Clearing negativity by visualizing rivers of light

If you wish to practice "inner world feng shui," you can empower what you do in the physical realm with powerful mental visualizations. The easiest mental imaging I know, and the one that gives the fastest result, is that involving visualizations of light flowing like rivers.

Spend some time practicing first. The best way to get an idea of how to do this is by looking at a city at night from a high vantage point, as from a descending aircraft. Notice how the roads and cars appear as rivers of light moving along it. This is a very powerful image, but now you must be in control of the light river. It should be a benevolent light, bright but not glaring. Start by imagining flowing white light.

Imagine a river of floating candles, or streams of fiberoptic lights, to clear negative mental clutter.

Focus on your door
Stand outside your home in your garden and focus on the main entrance. Make sure the door is open. The best time to do this is early on a bright morning. Close your eyes and imagine the sun as a throbbing, pulsating ball of very powerful, nourishing white light. Do not look directly at the sun; its brightness could blind you. Just feel its presence in the sky and visualize it in your mind.

Bring in the light
Imagine that it is sending out a river or strand of light from the sky, and feel this flow of light moving slowly and benevolently into your home. Envisage this river, the instant it enters, lighting up the house with precious yang essence, bathing all of its interiors with its glow.

This is a very powerful clearing visualization and, when imbued with powerful concentration, the home will instantly feel lighter. The drowsiness of its inhabitants vanishes. Anger dissipates. Feelings of despondency and fear evaporate. The sun is a very empowering catalyst; it is possible to learn how to harness its energy for the home using nothing more than the power of the mind. When you perform this visualization, you will feel a glow of companionship and love around you. It's a good idea to do it any time you feel flat about your life or your family is going through a rough period.

How to utilize the earth energy of holy places   102

Earth energy is probably the most powerful of the five-element energies. I am especially conscious of this because like many people, I have walked on very sacred ground and felt the power of this energy pulse beneath my feet.

The earth of these holy places–especially holy grounds where many pilgrims go to say prayers and chant mantras–will have been energized for many years, even centuries, by people's prayers and mantras. Take some home with you–just a tiny bit will do–and sprinkle it on your garden, mixing it with the dirt of your back yard. My garden contains holy earth from many places of pilgrimage all over the world, and I believe that is one of the reasons why my plants are so lush, my flowers bloom all the time, and my fruit trees always bear fruit.

Tuning into the spirit of the earth

More important is that, in focusing my mind on the earth upon which my house is built, I am honoring the land beneath it. I also become aware of the power of my home's earth energy.

In the Southwest part of my garden, I have placed three large boulders to signify the trinity of earth, heaven, and Man. Those of you living in apartments can also place special boulders or semi-precious stones in the Southwest–they activate the corner with powerful earth energy. Place a red packet filled with coins (three, six, or nine coins) under the boulders to activate them, thereby creating powerful emanations of earth energy. If you know Flying Star feng shui, you can also activate the auspicious mountain star in the same way.

Any kind of stone–pebbles, small rocks, crystals, and large boulders–represent earth energy.

If you are able to, get some dirt from the home of a wealthy man. Mix his earth with yours, or put it into a small plastic bag and keep it to make your wealth vase.

These recommendations all activate earth energy to enhance "relationship luck." Not only in areas of marriage and family, they also enhance relationships with colleagues, superiors, and business associates.

Keep some earth from the garden of a rich man to promote wealth.

103 Ways to stimulate "growth chi" and "support luck"

More powerful than mere granite boulders are natural crystals and semi-precious stones that have been fashioned into smooth, small to medium-sized rocks. These simulate mountain energy and are extremely powerful for nurturing the earth corners of any home.

I am very fond of jade or green-colored stones that have been fashioned into tall, rectangular-looking rocks. These simulate powerful "growth chi." Entrepreneurs who

are building businesses would benefit from placing such a green-colored rock in their offices–either behind or in the Southwest or Northeast corners of them. It will bring them into contact with influential, useful business associates. The relationship luck generated thereby will benefit their businesses.

Precious and semi-precious stones create support luck–help from others.

Smooth rose quartz stones mounted on attractive redwood stands are very beneficial for love, while other earth-colored rocks attract the goodwill of many people.

If you want to create "support luck" of any kind, you should invest in one of these semi-precious stones. Indeed, with the growing interest in crystals, more and more rocks of this kind are now commercially available.

In the old days, the homes of mandarins and powerful court officials were decorated with beautiful precious stones. Not many of these antique rocks have come onto the market because, in China, it is believed that they should always stay in a family. But if you visit some of the museums in China, you will be able to see some old semi-precious stones that have graced the mansions of family homes for many years.

Rituals for cleansing rocks and crystals   104

If you bring any kind of earth-energy enhancers into your home–and these include rocks and crystals in any shape or form–you must remember that they are very powerful storers of energy, and that they contain both negative and positive charges. It is, therefore, advisable to cleanse them of negative energy that has been inadvertently picked up along their journey into your home. Refer to any good book on crystals and you will find several ways to cleanse these and semi-precious stones.

A mixture of sea salt and rock salt can be used to cleanse crystals.

One way to cleanse them is by placing them in the open air where they can take a sunshine or rain bath. This empowers them with the natural chi of the outdoors. This is, in fact, a better way to empower personal single-pointed crystals.

I carry most of my personal crystals with me whenever I go to the beach or the high mountains, because there the natural environment has clarity and possesses awesome energy. When you later return these crystals to your home, they will have stored all of that powerful natural energy inside them. When you shine a bright light on your crystals, this wonderful energy is released into your home. If you wish, you can give your rocks and crystals extra power via special mantras and/or empowerment symbols. When properly energized with relevant mantras written or chanted on them, these rocks and crystals dissolve whatever negative feng shui energies may be harming the harmony and relationships luck of people within your household. When you add the extra dimension of empowerment with special mystical symbols, their effect becomes even stronger.

In this book, I have included a chapter introducing the power of mystical symbols and showing how to use them to empower objects like rocks and crystals to benefit living spaces. Such energized rocks become powerful sources of "relationship chi," and bring good vibrations into a home so that relationships become extremely harmonious.

The seven-day cleansing ritual

I use a very simple cleansing ritual. I soak my rocks and crystals in a solution of sea and rock salt for seven days and nights. Salt is extremely effective at dissolving all traces of past energy. Like reformatting zip disks, salt wipes out all previous vibrations that may be stuck in rocks.

105 Preliminaries for energy empowerment

Dejunking your home goes beyond clearing clutter. Physical clutter represents just one layer of the home's energy matrix. To make a space a true haven for its residents, most homes need physical and spiritual cleansing.

Introducing spiritual housework

Regularly throwing away unwanted or redundant items is the first step on the path to spiritual space cleansing, but this first step is also a quantum leap—this is because the well-being of any home and its residents depends upon the quality of a home's auric field. The auric field always needs cleansing so that all negative, dead, or killing energy never accummulates to a level where it threatens inhabitants with adversity and misfortune.

Everything to do with the spatial cleansing of negative, harmful energy fields always begins at the physical level. Discarding unwanted physical objects and possessions releases stagnant and negative energy and kick starts the energy of the home. Yet when the physical clutter has been removed, there is often residual negative energy that needs clearing, and for this you need to practice cleansing the psychic dimension—or spiritual housework (see Tip 107).

This can be followed by simple empowerment rituals (see Tip 110) that enhance the positive glow of the home's auric field. These also boost the energy of the home, making it a safe sanctuary, and a very auspicious, harmonious place to live, where residents prosper to a ripe old age.

Where to start

There are three basic preliminaries to observe in order to purify and empower a home's auric field. It is vital to observe these preliminaries before engaging in work that borders on the spiritual, as psychic work on energy fields is invisible and intangible. Energy cannot be seen; it has to be felt and sensed. Before using empowerment techniques to enhance and improve the quality of a home's energy, it is important to observe the basic preliminaries before you begin.

The Three Steps to Heavenly Housework

1. **Establishing determination:** setting your intention and your dream for a harmonious environment (see Tip 106)

2. **Psychic housework:** Using incense, sound, and visualization techniques to purify your spiritual space (see Tips 107, 108)

3. **Completion rituals:** Dedicating your psychic housework to your home's inhabitants (see Tip 109).

Establishing determination   106

The stronger and more focused your motivation, the more successful you will be. There is nothing difficult about establishing proper motivation. It requires neither mantras nor prayers. Becoming conscious of why you are doing something merely reinforces in your mind what you want from your home, and usually invokes powerful feelings and determination within you to get on with the job. It also enables your conscious intention about your purpose to merge with your subconscious intention. In short, establishing your motivation is in itself very empowering.

What about expectations?

Never be too obsessive about your expectations. There is much to be said for taking a relaxed attitude toward psychic space cleansing. Like practicing feng shui, the more relaxed and less uptight you are, the higher your chances of success. Don't keep worrying about what you may be doing wrong. Go with your own inner flow of energy and have faith and confidence in your own innate abilities. Remember that we are all blessed with the ability to communicate directly with the energy that swirls around us. The simple act of focusing the mind is like pressing the "on" button. This is because consciously engaging the mind is like giving it permission and direction to touch the intangible energy fields of our very existence.

In recent years, a great deal of work and research has been directed towards learning about these energy fields. As a result, much new information is emerging and being used with great success in healing work—healing that repairs the energy fields of the physical body and the mental-auric field of the mind, as well as the auric field of space and time.

At a practical level, take an immediate to short-term approach to the psychic cleansing of your space, but also specify in your mind what your long-term goals are. Spend a few moments thinking about the different methods that are contained in this book, and determine which rituals you want to use. Remember that clearing clutter in different rooms has already started the chi moving in your home and that psychic space cleansing is simply taking the exercise a step higher into the spiritual auric realms of the house. It makes the cleansing go deeper so that the effects of the whole dejunking exercise last longer.

Once you generate your motivation strongly, the rest will be easy. With the journey already started in the mind, action flows smoothly.

Checklist

1. Get powerful—think about what you really want from your home and your life. Write this down if it helps you to focus.

2. Go beyond—think of this mental process in the same way you consider discarding physical junk. Establishing your determination is the first step in taking the decluttering process to the next level.

3. Everything begins with a thought, idea, or conversation. Consider this, and see where it leads you. Accept what your dreams are right now, not what you think they should be, and you'll be on the right path.

107 Undertaking psychic house cleansing

There are many different methods used for psychic cleansing. You can use incense and sound cleansing, for example, or a combination of these with psychic cleansing rituals that you may be familiar with from other spiritual traditions. But if you are to make the cleansing powerful on a psychic level, it means that the rituals you do on a physical level must be accompanied by visualizations.

Visualizations engage the power of your mind and tap into what I refer to as the universal mind–the ultimate source of all knowledge, wisdom, and purity. They work in parallel with the mind, but at a more powerful level.

Psychic cleansing does not mean you must be still–you can use visualizations when physically cleaning to boost your home with even more energy.

How to sweep away negativity
Begin your practice by adding this psychic dimension while sweeping the floor at home.

As you sweep, visualize that you are sweeping away bad luck, negative attitudes, anger, and everything that may be causing frustration and anxiety to members of your household. With every sweep of the broom, visualize all of these negative things being swept out of your home. Think that you are using the power of the universal source to do this.

In the same manner, visualize all the negatives in your life, all the strain, tension, and problems being sucked up by the vacuum cleaner as you move around the room. As the vacuum sucks up all of the dirt on the ground, imagine that it is also sucking up everything that is causing you grief, stress, and aggravation.

How to soak up sadness with salt
For wiping the surfaces of tables, cupboards, shelves, and furniture, use rock salt in the cleaning water rather than soap or chemical cleansers. Psychic cleansing does not require chemicals. All it requires is a damp cloth soaked in natural salt and a visualization that all lingering negative energy is being sponged up by it, leaving surfaces clean of harmful or depressing psychic energies.

When you have mastered the art of visualizing this disposal of negative energies, you can start to use similar visualizations when cleansing space with incense or sound. For example, imagine that, with the ringing of a bell or the harmonics of a singing bowl, all intangible negative chi is absorbed by the sound and transformed into pleasant, fresh energy that brings happiness and joy into your house. Remember to seal your cleansing sessions with dedications (see Tip 109).

When to do psychic cleansing   108

Psychic cleansings can be spontaneous or elaborately scheduled, I tend to go with the flow, rather than plan ahead. Sometimes when I wake up in the morning and see signs that some psychic cleansing is needed, I do it.

What are these signs? I am alert to all sorts of small things going wrong. I may feel an urgent need to spread incense around the entrance of my home, and some signs may compound this feeling–the door gets jammed; I misplace my car keys; the computer breaks down; the dog knocks over the flowerpots. I see these little calamities as messages from the cosmos in the form of gentle reminders that there are things around me that need to be cleansed. When you become sensitized to your environment, you will be surprised how fast you notice these signals. Your home will actually "talk" to you through the manifestation of signs.

The communication is always symbolic. Sometimes signs indicate that negative energies are strong–for instance, you wake up with swollen eyes, the dog goes lame, the car bangs the garage door while you're backing out, you slip in the bathroom and cut yourself. These signs suggest that it's time to tune into the space around you and undertake some serious spatial clearing. Consciously tune into the auric field of your home so that you can identify any pockets of yin energy or corners where the chi may be stale and stagnant. Get used to being very receptive to the messages your home sends you.

Little accidents, from a broken flowerpot to lost keys, can signal an imbalance of energy in your home that needs attention.

Reasons to observe completion rituals   109

Each time you repair the energy and auric fields of your home by using powerful visualizations, you should spend a few minutes of your time dedicating the process to the inhabitants of your home–your family or your housemates. Making dedications conserves the energy in a place, and completes the process of space cleansing. This also seals in the value of what you have done so that its effects are longer lasting, and anything negative that might happen later is reduced in severity.

The regular psychic cleansing of homes does make a difference. Negative energy is banished and diluted. Like good feng shui, you may not see it working because it successfully stops something bad from happening; this is how the process works.

Medical doctors of the Chinese Emperors' courts were careful to practice preventive medicine, because they might well lose their jobs (or even their heads) if the Emperor ever became ill. Equally, feng shui advisers are expected to be able to make recommendations that prevent defeat, loss, and illness. The Chinese masters who make house calls to cleanse space after illness or death, for example, often burn small pieces of yellow paper on which are written special dedications, to end a ritual. You can do the same. Write down a general blessing wish for the house and its residents, such as "May all who live here do so harmoniously, and may prosperity come to them," and then burn the paper. The act of burning the paper seals the dedication in the house.

110   Psychic empowerment and the harnessing of chi

There are different ways of psychically empowering your home and the objects within it. I have been taught a few methods, which have enabled me to energize my personal jewelry, thereby turning my pieces into powerful amulets and talismans that have protective attributes. In the same way, the auspicious objects placed around my home are similarly empowered. Maybe this is why I am a great believer in symbols of good fortune; they work so magnificently for me.

Psychic empowerments are different from blessings. Empowerments involve the enhancing of energy auric fields–tapping into the universal source–while blessings invoke divine deities. There is a big difference in these two practices, and it is also one of intensity. Blessings are always more powerful than simple psychic empowerments. The most potent kinds of blessings come from highly realized lamas and yogis, although those from our parents and older people who have lived a good life, or by our teachers who have developed spiritual realizations, are also very powerful.

In Taoist institutions in Hong Kong, Taiwan, and China, that have older resident master teachers, disciples learn many valuable Taoist techniques of harnessing chi, and these are similar to psychic empowerments. These techniques are secrets since they are not universally known, although, in recent years, a great many of these precious teachings have become increasingly widely available. Taoist methods of energy empowerments are based on a proper understanding of chi, which is the life force. It is also the central essence of Taoist philosophy and magic. According to Taoist Masters, everything is chi and has chi.

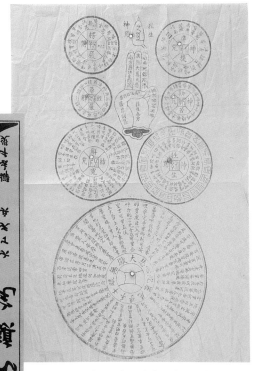

Taoist Masters have a knowledge of powerful symbols that they use when harnessing chi energy in rituals.

Chi and chi kung

The study of chi can be broadly categorized as chi kung, which is usually studied for health reasons. There are many different branches of chi kung. The most popular of those generally known today are physical exercises that involve breathing techniques that engage the chi within the human body. This kind of chi kung is excellent for maintaining good health.

Another kind of chi kung involves incorporating visualizations. This heightens one's awareness of nature, and also one's sensitivity to the quality of the chi that surrounds us. These are methods that enhance psychic consciousness and energy empowerments.

Finding a teacher to show you empowerment techniques   III

Many of the empowerment techniques are taught only to advanced disciples of chi kung, kung fu, or Taoism, that is, to those who have mastered physical exercises to a high level. Much of the teaching involves sitting and standing meditations, creative visualizations, and breathing. I was very lucky in that I had the good karma to be given the opportunity to learn the meditative techniques and the visualizations without having to go through the long period of apprenticeship mastering these physical exercises. I was warned that my body could suffer if I did the meditations under a state of stress or tension, as this would magnify their negative impact on my body. Having not perfected many of the physical movements and exercises, I was told that I should learn to at least relax my body and free it of all tension each time I sat down on the meditation mat in order to develop my mental imaging capability.

Learning to visualize

The key, I was told, was to be as relaxed as possible, as unstressed as possible. It is only when one has the ability to stay detached from one's surroundings, and not to get distracted, that one's visualizations take on clarity and strength. In the process, one also becomes able to access other dimensions of consciousness.

I discovered that simple meditative chi kung exercises that engage mental visualizations are well within the scope of everyone's capability. Finding a good teacher is very helpful. It is important to find a teacher who can impart some of the vast secrets of the kind of chi kung practice that borders on

Taoist magic. I myself have come across some great masters. Some have already passed on, since I came under their influence while still quite young, and the few exercises I learned from them in my twenties have served me well. Healthwise, the exercises I have learned have been marvelous in helping me maintain my youth and vigor. But I have also had the great good fortune to have come under the care of some highly realized yogis—master spiritual practitioners with highly developed meditation and visualization skills. I met my most impressive teacher in 1997. He is my very precious Buddhist master and guru, Lama Zopa Rinpoche. However, Rinpoche's teachings focus on cleansing the mind more than space, and the motivation behind his methods are geared towards generating the good heart that leads to enlightenment, rather than to creating material wealth.

What I did discover was that, in practicing more spiritual meditations, my ability to do psychic cleansing in my physical space took a quantum leap in effectiveness. So I strongly advise finding a teacher if you are keen to learn about energy empowerment.

Meditation and visualization practice under the guidance of a teacher boosts your ability to transform the atmosphere in your home.

112   Brightening the auric field of the human body

Everyone has the ability to sense energy or chi with their hands, and from thereon to receive and transmit energy to spaces and objects, and even to other people. This is how healing is done. For instance, it is possible to develop sensitivity in the hands to receive energy from the sun and the moon that will strengthen and brighten your personal auric field.

All that is needed is practice. Think of the human body as having three central columns of energy, and then think of circular forces rotating around the body from the head down to the toes. When you learn to receive energy from the sun or moon, it is transmitted to your auric field, strengthening it.

The more you think and visualize this auric field of your body, the more easily you will

be able to visualize similar auric fields around objects. Everything in the Universe exists with vibrational energy around it. Using your hands, you can then transmit energy to strengthen the auric fields of objects. Empowering energy work is done at the level of these auric fields so that, when you succeed in strengthening the positive yang side of these objects, they emit prosperity, positive, or protective chi in accordance with their symbolic meaning.

Once you learn this, you will be able to empower the auric field of your home as well as that of special objects inside it. This is an amazingly rewarding technique to use and apply to complement feng shui practice. Using visualization and working on the chi and auric fields is really inner feng shui practice and is very powerful.

You can learn to receive the positive energy from nature by sensitizing your body to the environment.

Sensitizing your hands   113

The first step to energy empowerment is to develop your hands' sensitivity to energy. This is done with a few simple exercises. In order to work with energy, you should also know how to capture, feel, and eventually transmit it. The hands are the best to work with because the surface of the palms are said to be the most sensitive to chi vibrations. Start by rubbing your hands together in an upward and downward motion–starting slowly at first, and then more vigorously. You will feel a warm sensation, a tingling, in the hands. This warmth is very beneficial for the eyes. Press on your eyes with your palms to feel the energy.

Energizing Your Palms

These exercises help to sensitize the palms of your hands:

1. Hold out your palms in front of you. Using your thumbs, rub your fingers so that the palms open and close. Do this about twenty times.

2. Rub your two palms together steadily until you feel warmth. Develop sensitivity to the smoothness or roughness of your palms.

3. Then, standing with your legs one foot (30 cm) apart, let your hands fall by your sides. With your palms facing the back, swing your arms lightly back and forth about twenty times as high as your hands will go without straining. Let your arms hang loose. This moves the chi around the body.

4. Now turn your palms to face your sides and beat the sides of your body lightly with both palms, up and down, up and down, twenty times. Feel the swing in your arms. This moves the chi farther.

5. Finally, lift both palms in front of you, with palms facing each other, about 8 in (20 cm) apart. Keep your palms facing each other this way for about one minute. By now you will be able to feel the chi between your hands. Slowly move your palms outward to feel the expanding chi, then move your palms inward to feel the contracting chi. Like holding a ball between the hands, imagine the ball expanding and contracting.

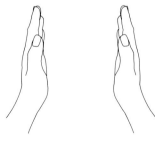

If you do not feel the chi immediately, practicing this for several days should do it. Once you are able to feel the chi, you will be ready to receive and send out energy with your hands. You will be able to start doing simple energy empowerments. The more you practice, the more sensitive your hands will become.

114   Using your hands to send and receive energy

Practice sending and receiving energy with your hands until you get them used to the sensation of energy. Different people feel the energy of the cosmos that surrounds us in different ways. Not everyone feels the tingling sensation; some feel energy as being warmer and others feel a sensation that is impossible to describe. Most people are not aware they have the ability to receive chi from the sun, moon, plants, trees, flowers, and so forth. Energy can be either negative or positive, and our hands are sensitive to both. Whether we receive the energy or not is decided by the thought processes. Only when the mind tunes in to the energy and concentrates on receiving it will the energy be transmitted.

So, once you have sensitized your hands, practice listening to the energy of your home. Place both of your palms flat on its walls, slowly moving along them in an anti-clockwise direction. This brings out past energy, and if you listen to the energy, you will begin to absorb the feeling transmitted by it. Good energy is usually joyous, while negative energy transmits fear, anger, and depression. Go around the walls of each room at least once, in order to get a feeling for the energy.

Singing bowl

Wooden mallet

Complement space cleansing with protection symbols such as the Chinese Pi Yao.

How to Clear the Air

If you feel exhausted, the energy is being taken from you by your surroundings. Your home is hungry for fresh yang energy. Give it an air and sunshine bath by opening all the doors and windows for a while and by turning on bright lights at night for a few hours at least.

If you feel angry, frustrated, depressed, or experience any kind of negative emotion, your home's energy badly needs cleansing. There may be too much residual energy left over from some previous argument or showdown. You should undertake spatial cleansing with a singing bowl and wooden mallet (see Tip 69).

If you feel fear rising within you, the energy of your home is being subjected to killing chi. Look around for poison arrows that you may have missed–sharp pointed edges, hostile pictures, or clashing color schemes. Use a singing bowl to clear the space quickly as an interim measure, and then invest in images of protective and celestial creatures such as Fu dogs, Chi Lins, Pi Yaos, tortoises, and dragons. These are able to diffuse killing chi.

If you feel nauseous, or you suddenly get a tummy ache, or a headache, then this is a sign that there is sickness chi around. For this, you need to use incense to cleanse the space.

Creating the blue-light cocoon for protection 115

Those of you familiar with creative visualization, or those who have done some meditation, will find it easy to mentally create a force field.

1. First, stand in the center of a room. Raise both arms high in front of you, with palms open and facing outward. Take a deep "in" breath as you raise your arms, then gently lower the palms of your hands a few inches. Breathe out. Do this three times to awaken the chi. Visualize receiving energy in the form of golden light from the universe.

2. Hold your hands, palms open, facing the sky as if to receive energy from the universe. Feel the chi by tuning into the palms of your hands. Stay like this for a few minutes. When you feel a tingling sensation on your palms, slowly turn them to face each other. Your hands are still high above your head.

3. Slowly lower your hands, imagining holding a transparent sphere of protective blue-tinged light between the palms of your hands. Hold this sphere of bright intense energy.

4. Next, move your palms very slowly away from each other and imagine the sphere of light growing larger and larger. Now visualize the sphere of light energy becoming brighter and bigger until it becomes bigger than you, bigger than the room, bigger than your house, your apartment – until soon its protective light.surrounds the whole house or apartment building. Nothing negative can penetrate the force field created by this sphere of light.

5. Focus strongly on this protective aura around your home. Be convinced of its power. Now gently visualize the blue light completely cocooning your house, apartment, or room. Think, "This is the energy field of my space/home/room. Nothing harmful can penetrate this energy field." It helps to have a picture of your home in your mind, over which you see the cocoon of blue light. Think of this cocoon of light as a protective halo around your home.

116 Creating a force field of protective chi

Before undertaking any kind of energy empower- ment work, get used to creating a defensive field of guardian chi around the house. This ensures that, should you be disturbed by any noise or distracted by wandering entities, they will not be able to pene- trate your light cocoon. It is like building an invisible shield that defends the home so that its energy will not succumb to attacks from hostile chi. This is done by developing your ability for focused visualization. Everyone has this ability, to mentally create powerful visualizations. The images you build have a mysteri- ous power and this can be channeled towards creat- ing a force field of energy that protects the home.

This force field defends the home in different ways. First, it prevents hostile chi from penetrating the nat- ural aura of your home; it stops anyone with hidden bad intentions towards the residents from even entering the home; and it acts as an invisible barrier against wandering spirits who coexist with us in a different realm. The power of the force field that you build will depend on the strength of the concen- tration you use to create it. Generally, the more attuned you are to the energy of your home, the closer you will be to its spirit and, therefore, the more empowered your force field will be. An affinity with the spirit of your home empowers your visual- izations with tremendous strength. Empowerment of this kind can never be used to harm; it works best when your motivation is pure–for instance, when parents are motivated to protect their children, their mental visualizations carry great strength. This is because the energy behind the mental image is un- conditional love, the spirit of which has great power.

117 Another way to create blue-light protection

Visualize a halo of blue light above your home, with the halo sending protective beams of light onto it down below. In this method, the protective field is emanating from above the home, rather than surrounding it.Both this and the method described in Tip 115 are as effective as your mind makes them. They are excellent ways of protecting your home at night when everyone is sleeping, and for protection against theft and fire. When you practice these visu- alizations regularly, your home will enjoy a wonder- ful serenity–the kind of harmony that comes from being one with the cosmos. This is because you are actively drawing vital energy from the universe and channeling it into your home, making it vibrant and filled with strong yin-yang chi, which is also the universal tai chi. Do this mental imaging exercise regularly. You will be astonished at how good you become after just a week of visualization exercise.

If you live in an apartment, you can imagine a cocoon of blue light encasing the whole building so that everyone residing within will also enjoy the benefits of your magnificent visualization. Stand in front of the apartment building and soak in a picture of the whole building into your subconscious before doing the protective visualization.

Practice with a determined and focused concen- tration; remember that you are not using your own energy to empower your home with protective chi– you are using energy drawn from the cosmos. So you need never be afraid of ever becoming exhausted with this exercise. At all times, make certain that you are not tense. The great secret of success in visualization work is the ability to generate a relaxed awareness of the subconscious being attuned to the cosmos.

A grounding ritual at the hour of the dragon 118

The home also draws a great deal of its strength and vigor from the ground on which it is built. Whenever the energy of the home grows tired, or is strained through the excessive buildup of yin energy inside it, one powerful method of re-energizing the home is by drawing energy from the ground. Imagine that your home has a grounding cord, which resembles a vast tubular root, connecting its center to the bowels of the earth. Think of it as being a thick root that goes deep into the ground and sends thousands of little roots outward that soak up energy from the earth and then bring it up to the home.

This is a very powerful visualization for revitalizing the energy of your home. It draws powerful earth chi into the house and is especially good for enhancing relationship luck for all of its residents. Visualize the root going deep into the ground and drawing forth powerful earth energy into the home. Think of it as a grounding cord that has the ability to balance the chi of your home, adding strength and vigor to its foundational energy.

This empowerment is excellent when you feel that the world is against you, when you feel unloved and in need of friends. It creates very comforting energy for you when you are going through a depressing period or when you are having more than your fair share of relationship problems and politicking woes at the office.

The grounding cord empowerment should be done in the early morning during the hour of the dragon, between 7 and 9 am. This is when the visualization is most potent.

At the same time, also look at the immediate vicinity of the home. Make sure there are no trees too close to the home. If there are, ensure that their leaves and foliage don't over-shadow the home to the extent that the life-giving sun's energy is blocked out. Also, the roots of nearby trees will disturb the invisible grounding cord of the home, thereby causing its inhabitants to experience instability and imbalance. The result is a sudden loss of support from friends and colleagues alike. When you sense such a situation, just stand in front of your home in the early morning, take a deep breath and, holding both hands stretched out in front of you, visualize a very bright yellow light at the base of the center of your home. Visualize the grounding cord filling up with yellow light and follow it with your mind all the way deep down into the earth. In your mind, "see" the roots light up as your mind touches them with your consciousness. Then feel energy surging upward toward your home, stabilizing and centering it.

Spend some moments establishing your mental image of your home with its grounding cord lighted up in an array of lights just like the pattern of roots growing deep into the earth.

Think: "I am empowering our home with grounding earth energy. This restores the stability in our home, bringing powerful relationship luck back into our lives."

Dragon symbol with accompanying calligraphic translation.

119 Tuning in to the guardian spirit of the home

All homes have guardian spirits. These are different from entities or parasites from another cosmic dimension. The spirit of the home is not an entity, not a ghost, and certainly not a deity. You do not need to think of it as such. The spirit of the home just is. When the spirit of the home is happy, a happiness aura pervades it, and when it is unhappy, it, likewise, sends out desolate and unhappy vibrations.

So it is a good idea to think of the spirit of the home as the sum total of its energy, reacting to the events and the people who occupy it. Few people realize that the spirit of a home takes its cue from its inhabitants, and that the sum total of the combined energy vibrations emanated by these residents plays a very big part in determining the quality of the home's energy.

For example, when residents allow their anger to frequently explode into violent verbal battles, the home becomes angry. When one fierce tyrannical patriarch who is the most compelling person in the home dominates everyone else, the energy within the home will be dominated by feelings of fear. It is because of this human influence on spatial energy that prisons have such horrible energy; why hospitals are filled with sickness chi; why police stations are dominated by a rough, violent feeling.

Homes have personalities

Buildings do take on the energy of their occupants. The flow of chi-influences mirrors the dominant chi of their residents. When you tune into the guardian spirit of buildings, they encapsulate the combined energies of feelings put forth by residents within them. A happy home has a happy spirit. A joyous air attracts positive vibrations, while a despondent atmosphere attracts negative reactions and outcomes.

Space cleansing cannot stop at the spatial cleansing of the physical home alone. It is necessary, even vital, to clear the negative clutter that resides in the mind. When you do, you rid yourself and your environment of all aggravations, stresses, and tensions that cause the creation of excessive negative chi.

A home can be decorated with symbols that sum up its spirit. This is obvious if the location of your home is characterful–a waterside residence may display nautical prints and decorative shells that echo the presence of a protective spirit.

Dejunking the mind of clutter   120

Alas, we have so much clutter inside our heads, collected through the years, consciously and unconsciously, along the journey of life. We store junk-thoughts in the mind's various compartments from the moment we are born and, because the mind has an all-powerful supercharged storehouse capability, we are not aware of all the surplus information stored within. Over time, we accumulate sad experiences that reinforce negative attitudes. These do little good to our sense of well-being and state of mind. Depressing memories that are reinforced over time lead to frustration, anger, jealousy, harmful attachments, stress, and possibly fears and phobias. We will be happier as individuals if we reduce the intensity and quantity of our mental garbage and, even better, eliminate it altogether. This will result in a lightening of the load that confuses the brain, and negates our ability to remain rational, composed, and happy.

What leads to mental decluttering?
Mental junk needs clearing even more than physical junk. But clearing physical junk is what starts the overall dejunking process that affects the mind. It acts as a catalyst.

Thousands of volumes have been written about the memory storehouse of the human mind, including research into our retentive capability, the conscious and subconscious, the way we recall and use information, and, most importantly, how our behavior and attitudes are directly and indirectly influenced by everything we have ever experienced, seen, heard,

learned, and digested. It is believed that the mind is so powerful that it forgets nothing. And if we believe all that is currently emerging about past lives and people's memories of them, it seems that the mind also does not forget anything it has experienced in other lives. This means that it is not easy to clear negativity from the mind.

Moreover, when we consider the sheer volume of information stored here—experiences, feelings, attitudes—surely what we have in our homes is really nothing when compared to the clutter inside our minds.

Ritual for Mental Dejunking

Close your eyes (without falling asleep) and tune into your mind. Observe the thoughts that flow through it. Watching the mind will make you aware of the number of random thoughts that weave their way in and out of your consciousness. Do this each time you feel angry, frustrated, or stressed. Do it each time the name of someone important to you crops up, or an issue you are debating is being discussed. Watch your mind and get a feeling for what's inside it. Try this also while trying to study, work, or concentrate. You will be surprised at the amount of junk-thoughts that interrupt your thinking. Dejunking the mind of negative and irrelevant thoughts enhances concentration and reduces your tension and fears. Make a conscious decision to do this, because it will bring emotional liberation that leads to a less stressful and aggravating life.

Every day we absorb a barrage of useful and useless information that accumulates as negative mental clutter.

121 Ditch your victim and loser phobias

So many of us have phobias related to the fear of failing. It is what I term "loser phobia." Closely allied to this is the fear of being the victim, of being "had" or conned. Fears are actually the sum of all the junk, or negative experiences stored in our minds. Doctors and advanced clinical researchers have discovered that so-called irrational phobias are rooted in past traumas buried deep inside the hidden recesses of the mind. Similarly, physical reminders of disturbing past episodes in our lives–things we keep hidden deep in drawers, dressers, and dark corners–are connected to memories that we appear, on the surface, to have forgotten.

Two of humanity's greatest fears–fears that seem to be the root cause of so many other fears–are those related to being a victim or loser. These root fears block us from relating to our higher selves. They rob us of our vitality to reach for the skies. They hold us back from who we are and who we can be. Fear of losing and fear of being a victim are major blockages to success. If we do not clear our minds of subconscious memories that reinforce these fears within us, we will go through our lives forever afraid of taking a leap of faith into the unknown.

Ritual for Moving On

Try to get rid of your defensive mechanisms.

1. Be conscious of the patterns of your reactions and responses to people and situations, then consciously take a deep breath, smile to yourself, and let go!

2. Say to yourself, "There is no need to yell, cry, get upset or mad–no need at all. There is no need to fear, no one to blame, and it is unimportant who is right and who is wrong. I am now aware of the situation and I shall cope simply because I can."

3. If you do this often enough, you will clear away a great deal of negative, harmful behavior. Try it and be pleasantly surprised about how quickly difficult situations are diffused.

The effects of "victims" and "losers"

Victim and loser phobias sabotage relationships and make people behave in self-destructive ways. Study the way you react to situations of failure and things that go wrong. Note the way you interact with friends and with aggravating people in your job. Be aware of what irritates you, or makes you defensive or withdraw. If you find yourself constantly looking for someone to blame, you are suffering from victim phobia. If you constantly feel obliged to explain, or habitually go on the defensive by complaining loudly, even about small things, you could be suffering from loser phobia.

Past experiences can act as negative emotional clutter which may lead us to act out victim or loser roles as adults.

Cleansing the mind of attitude clutter   122

The biggest hurdle to clearing the mind of harmful negative phobias is the self-realization that must precede the clearing. Once you think things through in your mind and are able to admit to your fears, there is seldom a need for anyone else to be aware of, or even to participate in, your mental clearing exercises. However, there will be those who will benefit from a guide or therapist who, through directed thought processes, can lead you to admit that you do have fears, which will simply evaporate once you realize you have them.

Clearing attitude clutter

Like spiritually charged negative energy, which takes so much effort to dislodge and cleanse completely, behavioral phobias are also deeply entrenched in you and therefore, cannot be cleared from your mind overnight. However, once you begin to become self-aware, accepting your vulnerability allows the cleansing of attitude clutter to get underway. Fear of pain, anger, rejection, and frustration become part of life and living. Difficult situations and relationships become things not to be feared but ones to be managed and overcome. Looking at relationships and situations this way requires a shift in attitude, and this can happen only when negative self-destructive attitudes are thrown away, eliminated, discarded and washed off.

Getting a yang attitude

Attitude is something that can apply to every single thing that happens to us. The yin and yang of attitude is but the two faces of the same situation, the same person. It is entirely up to us which side we want to see and react to, and which side of our attitude

A yang attitude encourages friendships based on openness and positivity.

we want to react with. Even when we see the situation or person we are interacting with as yin, we can still react positively in a yang way. When we make a habit of always reacting in a yang manner, we are setting up a yang bonding pattern for the future and discarding the yin bonding pattern.

Yang bonding patterns are very revitalizing. They open doorways to opportunities and positive relationships. Yin bonding patterns, on the other hand, close the doors to these developments. They create enemies and make situations worse. They cause more clutter to build up within the mind, clutter that reinforces self-destructive responses and bonding patterns.

123   Getting rid of self-destructive behavior

Self-destructive behavior is what we do when we push people away. It is when we play games with people, toying with their feelings, pushing them to the edge, seemingly insensitive to their unhappiness. In playing the game sometimes, we forget that every action of ours brings forth an equal and opposite reaction. The junk-perceptions within us make us behave in this self-destructive manner.

What is ego-junk?

This arises from the egotism of self-aggrandizement. I have seen so many super professionals reach heights of attainment and achievement only to self-destruct when they allow the clutter of their own rhetoric to blind them to reality. These are people who let the euphoria of attainment pump such quantities of junk into their minds that they lose their original clarity.

In recent years, we have seen the phenomenon of the humbling of celebrated CEOs—what the Economist magazine calls "the fallen idols"—where strikingly successful superheroes of the business world have destroyed themselves because they forgot to clear their heads of the clutter of jargon and rhetoric surrounding them. They have believed their own PR and publicity machines, forgetting what brought them success in the first place and completely swamped by the millions of words of praise heaped upon them. Many celebrities succumb to this kind of mental-junk buildup. When their minds become overloaded with bilge, they cannot cope with the weight of the stuff and are unable to discriminate between good and bad, nor tell who their

Even those who are successful with opulent lifestyles need to be mindful of ego-clutter—as accolades and beautiful artifacts accumulate, so does mental junk.

real friends are. Clutter has a way of creating massive confusion, indeed.

Junk can take many forms, but the worst is when it causes self-destructive behavior. So be wary of excessive praise. Beware of allowing too much meaningless rhetoric get into your head. Stay grounded. As I suggested you do for your home, create a grounding cord that keeps you firmly on the ground, not up in the air. When you fly too high, you can go beyond the force of gravity so that you are unable to feel the weight of the clutter inside your head. In this state of mind, you could self-destruct.

Dejunking the "alone" syndrome–adopt a pet   124

Some people suffer from what I call the "alone" syndrome. They usually have been solitary for so long that they fill their heads with thoughts of being alone, of being unworthy of being loved, of being convinced they are not attractive enough, not beautiful enough, not interesting enough. People like this give up on love and usually suffer from the secret, weighty, depressive consequences of low self-esteem. They may be thunderingly successful in their professional lives but when it comes to another human being, they protect themselves behind invisible walls. It can be very sad for them.

In the past, this kind of attitude was summarily dismissed as a lack of interest in the state of marriage. But in recent times, it has been recognized as a particular type of syndrome–a behavioral pattern that is repeated due to some deep-seated trauma that convinces the sufferer that he or she is meant to be alone, destined to be alone, or better off being alone.

The Spaniel and the Spinster

I have personally shaken this feeling from a good friend who was convinced that she was physically ugly and destined to go through life a spinster. She was brilliantly clever and a fabulously successful fund manager who was worth her weight in gold to the firm she worked for. But it seemed to me that she clung to her career success with such intensity to camouflage intense loneliness. In a sense, she had pulled down a window shade to protect herself from rejection and thus unconsciously drove people away. She found it hard to develop any kind of non-professional relationship with anyone, especially men. Indeed, she yearned desperately to find a soul mate, to get married, start a family, and bring some semblance of domesticity into her life. Yet she suffered from the alone syndrome so acutely that she would push away anyone who threatened to come too close.

So I tried a feng shui solution. I figured she needed yang energy in her home, so I presented her with an adorable golden long-haired spaniel–the kind of dog you cannot help loving. The change in her was astonishing. Not long after the pet entered her

household, she transformed into someone else. She literally came to life at the office. There was warmth in her voice and a softening in the way she spoke to everyone. The lovely little spaniel loved her to distraction. For the first time, she realized she was lovable and that she could love. Needless to say, it broke through the alone syndrome that had kept her imprisoned. It was not long afterwards that she met someone special and they set up home together. Later she admitted to me that Jasper (her spaniel) had made her confront the junk she had built up in her head about love.

Caring for a pet generates yang energy, helping to break down defenses and bring in love.

125 Shrugging off emotional baggage

We are each plagued with different emotional baggage–mental attitudes and prejudices that grip us tightly and make us react in negative ways to people and situations. Each of us has pet peeves, hang-ups and individual forms of dislike for certain people, places, and circumstances. These make up our emotional baggage, which, at its most harmless, is occasionally annoying and, at worst, causes anger and grudges that may last a lifetime. Emotional baggage takes the form of unforgiven slights and insults, the holding of grudges, the clenching of fists, and the remembrance of betrayal. I am constantly amazed at the depth of feeling attached to heavy emotional baggage,

Emotional baggage can build up over the years, becoming heavier and harder to bear.

and I wonder how anyone can bear the weight of carrying it for so many years. How much lighter it is not to carry such baggage. How much simpler it is to allow the memory of betrayal, abuse, insults, or slights to evaporate.

Do not be fooled by the demagogues who encourage you to keep your anger fueled. This will only add to the negative baggage you are carrying. Storing negative ideas like this leads to their escalation over time, as the mind will create many different kinds of imagined wrongs and multiply enemies. Get rid of this kind of junk before it dominates. Emotional baggage can explode into tragedies with major consequences. It is better to shrug it off your tired shoulders.

126 Clearing your life of aggravating friends

Just as you can clear the junk in your living space and your mind, you can with equal ease clear your world of junk-friends. You do not need the aggravation created by those who constantly put you down, discourage you, and depress you with the negative way they react to the things you do and say and the decisions you make. (After I made a conscious effort not to surround myself with people who made me feel unworthy and unlovable, my life took a quantum leap in happiness.)

Remember that the support groups you build around you add to the energy of your life. Negative people compound the negative things in your life. Judgmental friends turn everything into a battle. Surround yourself with friends who bring out the best in you, remind you of past triumphs, make you smile with self-assurance and feel you can achieve

just about anything. Friends who rejoice in your moments of happiness add glitter to your life.

When parents and teachers press down our spirits with their negative judgments, we have to learn to cope, but when we become adults ourselves we can choose who we want to have around us; there is never a need to put up with people who make us feel we are less capable than we are, and judge our lives by their own standards. You really can choose who you want to associate with, mix with, go out with. So from the start, make a conscious effort to cleanse the social environment with which you surround yourself. Get rid of friends who make you feel bad. This is social clutter of the most destructive kind. There is no bad chi like the bad chi of negative, judgmental people. If you want to feel better about yourself and your life, get rid of social clutter.

Eliminating negative emotions – emotional healing retreats

127

One of the most important aspects of clearing the clutter of your space–both physical and mental–is that of dealing with unresolved past hurts and old beliefs that stop you from moving forward. These include dysfunctional habits of behavior that once may have been useful and served you well in another earlier situation, but which now cause you distress. Another way of approaching this is to consciously look towards healing yourself emotionally of traumas and situations that may be causing you discomfort and grief. Identify them and then get rid of self-limiting attitudes so that you will be free to move forward. If you can liberate yourself emotionally from what holds you back, then you will be able to live freely in the present and savor the abundance of your present situation.

How retreats work

One of the best ways to heal yourself emotionally is to go on retreat. A retreat provides you with the opportunity to review patterns of thinking and acting that may be blocking you from living more fully in the present. It is when you are alone, far from your desk at work and your family, that you will be able to sift through what has happened in your life over the past ten years, and sort through everything you have accumulated, both in terms of material goods as well as all the habits of mind and behavior that have become the "you" that the world sees.

Clutter-clearing retreats make you go through your accumulation of positives and negatives, and to confront all the issues you may have pushed to one side and ignored; all the family and friends you have simply

avoided for no reason other than that you were too busy to remember their existence. Powerful emotional healing can take place when you are far from familiar home ground. Separated from your normal support systems, your inner self is allowed to rise and surface. Often the first few days of a retreat are hard. Negative things must surface for emotional healing to occur, and they are often painful. I discovered that the key is to simply observe your internal struggles. When anger and agitation arise in you, just back off.

Think of the process as laundering clothes. At first, all the dirt comes out and the water grows muddy but, as more dirt is washed away, the water clears and runs clean. It is the same with emotional cleansing. The process has to be difficult before things get better, has to be muddy before true clarity emerges.

Healing can work physically and mentally. As therapies such as massage help the body release and eliminate toxins, so emotional healing retreats encourage the release of old attitudes and negative memories, decluttering and purifying the mind.

128 Affirmations to re-energize self-esteem

I have been a firm believer of affirmations for as long as I can remember. Early on, I discovered that if I wanted something to happen badly enough, if I kept saying it, repeating it and thinking about it in a positive way, it would miraculously manifest. In the same way, if I wanted to develop a certain skill or ability, I would single-mindedly affirm my desire in my mind, and somehow situations would conspire for me to acquire the knowledge or experience I yearned for.

This was how I found myself the owner and chairman of my own department store in Hong Kong during the mid-eighties. I had discovered that I had a weakness for shopping and I realized that shopping was fun only when one has loads of money. But my subconscious mind was smarter. It propelled me into packaging the kind of investment banking deal I had been doing for years as part of my job, to enable me to acquire a department store. For two years, I shopped like an empress for my thirteen stores. It was amazing. When I tired of that life, I cashed in by selling out.

Using affirmation cards each day helps create positive energy.

Later, when I discovered mantras and found that yogis and lamas spend their lives chanting holy mantras in their quest for a transformation of the mind, and for enlightenment, my belief in affirmations was strengthened a thousandfold. Since then, I have turned my affirmations towards less material goals and more towards spiritual empowerments. I am also very keen now to transform my mind

If you want to empower your own aura, it is vital to have a healthy sense of self-esteem— a belief in your ability to have faith, to trust, to love, and to have respect for others in a non-egotistical way. Self-esteem arises from positive thought mantras directed at making others feel good, and from affirmations that create a feeling of being comfortable with who you are.

Letting go of fear

Fear must be eliminated—fear of hurting the self's ego. Once there is no more fear, everything else that is negative will evaporate. You will no longer attract negative people or negative situations into your life because you are comfortable with what and who you are. You will not even see anyone or anything as negative, and so your personal aura will become empowered. Then you will attract loving, positive people into your world. Happiness is then well within your reach.

So use thought and word affirmations to clear away all the clutter that surrounds your ego. Accept yourself for who and what you are, throw away all that makes you scared, defensive, angry, attached, and envious— and settle comfortably into your own skin.

Let go of the past and move on   129

Clearing mental clutter is something we have to do for ourselves. It cannot be delegated to someone else. This is because the clearing of deep-seated mental junk has a lot to do with your own core value systems. It is a very personal matter. No one can do mental clearing for you, not even professional therapists who may be experts in psychology and well-experienced in healing work.

At the crossroads of your life, unless you are prepared to let go of past beliefs and value systems that may be blocking your path forward and harming your potential for success, unless you are prepared to discard attitudes that are irrelevant and redundant in your present circumstances, you cannot

make way for new ideas and fresh energy to enter your consciousness. As you move from one stage of your life to the next, accept that transition times can appear uncertain and even be a little unstable. It is a fact of life that every turning point requires that mental trade-offs be made. It is a time when you will be forced to sift what is really important to you and what is not, and to clear out what is not.

Clearing mental clutter will always require you to let go of the past in order to move on. Be prepared to discard old ideas and belief systems that may no longer be relevant. Sometimes these may challenge your deep-rooted value systems. And then it is you who must decide.

When you feel choked, change the wall-art   130

The images you see on a daily basis have a very profound effect on your subconscious mind. Such images can be negative or positive, nurturing and empowering or exhausting and weakening. When you feel claustrophobic–choked up–as if you need more space to breathe, it is usually due to the effect of images disturbing your subconscious mind. You can take a holiday to get away from the routine of your life, or you can change the images that hang on the walls of your home. Art can be inspiring and give you a lift. But, over time, the same old paintings can become heavy and distracting. Change what hangs on your walls when you feel hemmed in.

Changing the ambience of your surroundings by changing the color and images with which you surround yourself is the best antidote for feeling that life is becoming too difficult. When you use this

cure, make sure you also change the dominant colors around you. Bring in lighter shades if you feel a need to expand and need extra vitality, and use darker shades if you feel a need to be more grounded.

Note that art is just a play of colors and images, and these have a powerful effect on your sense of well-being. Avoid hanging anything on your walls that suggests loss, or horror, such as distorted images, fierce animals, storms, fires, and portraits of old people. Instead look for open fields, blue skies, and calm waters. If you want to attract new experiences, invest in a painting with birds, for they are said to be the messengers of the cosmos. By bringing the image of a bird, or birds, into your home, you are sending out an invitation to the cosmos to manifest joyous new experiences in your life.

131 Strengthening your personal aura

The empowerment of the human aura is a spiritual exercise requiring intense mental concentration and visualizations. The strength of your auric fields has much to do with your mental, emotional, and physical health. It is affected by your moods as you react to external stimuli. Those who know about auras know that there are several auric layers that surround the human body. The aura is made up of translucent colors that change, lighten, and darken according to a multitude of stimuli like the weather, the person's mood, the energy of the surrounding space, or events. Most of all, the aura is affected by physical and mental health. It is possible to empower the aura. Your aura will be strong when you have a healthy body and mind. Illness drains the aura of its intrinsic strength, and robs it of its color. Toxins in the body exhaust the aura and make it weak.

Meditation and eating a healthy diet reduces internal and external stresses on the body, boosting your health and in turn your aura.

De-toxing

In recent years, many methods have been used to help the body detoxify. One way I have tried with great success is foot reflexology. I have regular sessions that help release toxins from my internal organs, which ensure I stay healthy. Reflexology works by enabling chi to flow freely throughout the body. Another way to do this is with the practice of simple chi kung exercises (see Tips 3, 6). As long as chi keeps moving through the body, the aura will stay strong and healthy.

I have spoken to some yogic practitioners and most of the time their humility prevents them from admitting to their siddhic powers. But I do know that they are powerful meditators and that their auras glow with a brilliance that is very divine. They tell me that it is important to lead a virtuous life to

strengthen the human aura. Stay pure, they tell me. Avoid causing harm to humans, animals, and all living creatures. Try not to become intoxicated or succumb to stimulants excessively they say, and occasionally, on special days, make some sacrifices to purify your body. Become vegetarian, or, better yet, fast for a day. Give the mind and body a chance to release the negative things inside them. And when you chant your purification mantras, they tell me, visualize that all toxins, spiritual harm, and negative thoughts that have accumulated since beginningless time are flowing out of the openings of your body as black ink, scorpions, frogs, and snakes. Think of yourself—your body and your mind—as being completely purified.

When your consciousness is purified, your aura glows. It becomes empowered. It strengthens.

Bathing in natural salt water to purify the auric field   132

Aless spiritual but nevertheless uplifting purification ritual is to bathe in natural salt water. An easy way to do this is to find yourself a beautiful beach and immerse yourself in sea water. This is a simple yet powerful way of neutralizing your body and mind of any spiritual harm caused to them and mental afflictions that may be making you feel depressed, weak, tense, and defeated.

Many of the old spiritual traditions believe strongly in the power of the sea bath. In Indonesia, one of the rituals for cleansing someone who is suffering from "spirit harm" (negative influences) is to immerse the person's whole body in the sea for seven successive days. It is believed that the sea has powerful neutralizing qualities for a broad variety of ills caused by imbalances in the spiritual persona. The salt crystals present in sea water are excellent for cleansing the auric field of impurities and afflictions that drain the human body of energy.

The next time you go for a beach holiday, select beaches that are less commercialized. Natural beaches where the waters have not been polluted are the best places to go for auric cleansing. The waters lapping up on unspoiled beaches are like high mountains. Their energy is pure and very powerful.

Avoid places where there is war and terrorism. Their presence and the frequent occurrence of killing and pillaging create very negative vibrations.

Cleansing and the number seven

The number seven is always significant in cleansing rituals. This is to correspond to the seven chakras or energy centers of the body and also the seven important planets that affect our well-being–the Sun, the Moon, Jupiter, Saturn, Mars, Venus, and Mercury. The Hindus add two more planets–Rahu and Ketu–to make nine planets. The Chinese also add two stars to the basic seven in many of their esoteric rites. Because of this, I sometimes go on for nine days when I undertake any kind of purification ritual. I also know of very serious practitioners who do it for seven times seven or forty-nine days.

A Cleansing Visualization

Remember to add this cleansing visualization to give your bathing ritual more potency. Think that, as you immerse in the water, all the tensions, aches, pains, grievances, stresses, and strains of your life are oozing out of your body through your pores and dissolving in the salt water.

Visualize waves carrying them far out to sea and shattering them into a zillion parts. If you can do this ritual along with powerful visualizations for seven days at the same time each morning, it will be very potent indeed. If seven full days is impractical, then do it seven times during one day.

133 The "yin water bath of the seven flowers" for purification

Taking purifying baths is a popular traditional ritual, which in recent years has been effectively incorporated into the relaxation services offered in spas and detoxification centers around the world. You too can incorporate such baths in your mental and physical cleansing processes.

The yin water bath

One easy purification bath is the "yin water bath of the seven flowers." When you bathe in yin-dominated water containing the seven flowers, you set the stage for what the sages refer to as the "zenith of yin." This is achieved by immersing your entire body in water that has been activated by seven different kinds of auspicious flowers. This ritual bath encourages the bather to grow calmer and become mentally detached from his surroundings.

In this ritual, the bather focuses on each different flower, using the petals of the flowers to focus his thoughts and turn off all thoughts about anything else. This visualization helps the mind relax. It tunes into itself and slowly transcends all aspects of routine behavior. This relaxed detachment allows yang chi to rise within the person. It can be mundane yang or celestial yang. When celestial yang rises but does not get dissolved and scattered by the mind's attachment to wandering thoughts, then it makes heaven chi unite with earthly chi; the result is a luminous soaring

upwards of yang energy. Then the bather truly feels centered and serene. This is regarded as magical bathing.

It is one of the best ways of making celestial yang energy rise to surround you with the essence of success. Select your flowers carefully to reflect and incorporate the colors of the five elements. Use more earth colors to strengthen relationship chi. Place greater emphasis on yellow and red flowers to strengthen the success aura. I like to recommend lots of yellow flowers, especially chrysanthemums, because they are very auspicious flowers and symbolize many good things–success, fame, and happiness. I also like white flowers like the magnolia and all the blossoms, especially the plum blossom and the cherry blossom, which signify longevity of good fortune. You can also choose jasmine, roses, and other fragrant flowers. In Bali, the spiritual island that really specializes in such baths, people like to use the frangipani, which signifies different kinds of good fortune.

Bath balls containing the essential oils of flowers that melt into the water as you bathe are a luxurious alternative to fresh blooms.

When you feel depressed, move the chi around 134

A sure fire way to strengthen your aura when you feel depressed is to move the chi in your immediate surroundings. This can be your office space if you are depressed about the state of things at the office, or your bedroom space if your depression is related to your love life, or any space where you spend much of your time.

Moving chi

Moving the chi does not involve doing anything very difficult. What is needed is for stationary objects like furniture–tables and chairs, planters and wall hangings–to be moved, shifted, or rearranged.

Moving office chi To move the chi in your office, get someone to help you move your desk–a few inches will be sufficient to move the chi. Anything moved more than 3 in (8 cm) will move chi. When you move a table a few inches to either the left or the right, or to the front or back, you will be setting in motion a whole series of changes in the way chi moves around you. When you move your table, you will also need to move your chair, so the flow of chi will change its pattern and set up a revitalized flow.

Moving wall chi If there are photographs, posters, or paintings hanging on the wall, take them down, give them a good clean and then put them back again. Try to put them back in a slightly different place, or move them around. You might retire them and get new pictures to decorate your walls.

Vibrant color and new wall-art shifts energy and revitalizes a room.

Spend an hour or so moving the chi. When you finish, you will be amazed at how much better you will feel. If there are planters and trees in your office, move them too. Moving plants is a very effective way to create new movements of chi. You can wind up your little session by looking around for things that should be thrown away–old pieces of paper, empty envelopes, old magazines and newspapers–so clear the clutter as well.

Moving bedroom chi Remove the mattress, wash the linens, and also move the bed. Give the space under the bed a good clean-up, getting rid of the cobwebs and bad dirt that have accumulated. You will be amazed at how much stuff you have under your bed. If possible, give the mattress and pillows a good outdoor sunshine bath. Nothing lifts depression like a strong dose of yang energy.

135 When you feel defeated, rearrange your desk

When you feel defeated, weak, and impotent–you will feel your energy and enthusiasm weaken considerably. We all go through horrible debilitating periods like this and it usually means that we are either very tired or our chi essence is exhausted. Most of the time, feelings like this are caused by your immediate work space. When you feel defeated, it is usually caused by some catalyst event. This can be a rejection, failure, disappointment, or someone yelling at, criticizing, or being unreasonable with you. Then everything around you will add to your sense of frustration.

At times like this, use feng shui to brighten your spirits and lift your confidence. See your work desk as a microcosm of the tai chi symbol (see Tip 141). View the desk as representative of the universal yin and yang essence as expressed in the Pa Kua symbol. Divide it into nine equal grids just like a Lo Shu square (see Tip 145) and, using your facing direction as the anchor direction, fill in this direction as the top center grid of your desk. If you are facing South, that grid is the South grid. The lower center grid (the one nearest you) will be the North grid. You can then fill in the directions for the rest of the grids.

The computer faces a good direction based on the user's Kua number.

Files are placed in the East.

Where to Start

Now rearrange all the things on your desk according to the following:

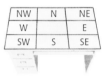

NW	N	NE
W		E
SW	S	SE

- Place your computer either on another side table on your right-hand side, or in the West or Northwest grid. If this is not possible, select a place where you are able to face one of your auspicious directions (based on the Kua formula).

- Set your files and In-tray on the East or Southeast grid. This should enhance your effectiveness in dealing with the matters inside the files.

- Put your Out-tray in the West in order to ensure that you will be protected no matter what decisions you make.

- Place lights in the South to gain the recognition of your superiors. A small candle burning here would also be quite powerful, or a lamp.

- Set a crystal paperweight in the Northwest of your desk to activate mentor luck. This will make your boss look favorably upon you. Placing a round crystal on your desk in the Northwest corner always creates strong "patronage luck."

When you feel unloved, bathe in a rainbow of colored lights

We all got through horrible moments of being convinced that no one cares or loves us. Even the most successful men and women are assailed by doubts about their self-worth. Moments like this descend on us for a whole variety of reasons; it is what makes the human race unique. Feelings of despondency have a range of causes.

I have discovered that trying to find root causes for such moments is of less help in dealing with them than doing something to counteract them. The most immediately revealing cure for despondency of this kind is to create a bath of rainbow-colored lights. The rainbow's seven basic colors cover an entire spectrum of cures that can be extremely healing.

A colored pendulum refracts light into rainbow colors. Each of these seven colors is associated with a particular type of healing that supports if you feel neglected.

Making rainbows

The easiest way to do this is to wrap a long filament light in strong rainbow-colored transparent paper. The colors on it should be red, orange, yellow, green, blue, lilac, and purple. In a darkened unlit room, turn on this specially prepared light and sit under it for about ten minutes. You then visualize the colored light beams shining down on you and entering your seated body through your crown chakra, at the top of your head (see Tip 31). It helps if you are relaxed and calm and able to see the lights entering your head as streams of color. In your mind, differentiate between each of the colors and focus on the meanings, which are listed in the box below. When you have focused on each of the individual colors, visualize all seven of them fusing into a single color—a dazzling white light. Do this by picturing the colors twirling and turning very fast until they merge into a single color. This white light is very powerful in bringing back confidence and love into your consciousness.

The Seven Benefits of the Seven Colors

Red	For courage and strength to believe in yourself
Orange	For taking the initiative in love
Yellow	For staying grounded in all of your relationships
Green	For calm acceptance for who you are
Blue	For love and waves of caring, nurturing energy
Purple	Fo receive confidence-boosting chi
Lilac	For spiritual upliftment that convinces you that you can cope with anything.

137 | When you feel weak, create sounds

When you feel weak and are convinced your life is stagnating, look for dust on your shelves and tune in to the yin chi that has obviously permeated your spaces. Yin energy can cause illness and various kinds of aches and pains. You experience an overpowering feeling of lethargy, which you simply cannot shake off. Sometimes you do not feel sick; you actually get sick, succumbing to viruses and allergies, and feel more vulnerable to diseases and physical afflictions, and your tolerance level retreats. It is not a nice feeling and the sooner you shake it off, the less chance it has of taking hold.

The benefits of sound therapy

There is no better cure for lethargy and weak chi in a house than sound therapy. Happy music played loud has a powerful way of sweeping away illness and weakness energy. Not all kinds of music and not all sorts of sounds are therapeutic, however. It is happy, light music that imbues an environment with strength. So play music that engages your heart and has a happy beat, which you can dance to and sing along with. It is the same with sounds. High sounds are more uplifting than low sounds. Bells, for

instance, work better than drums; the sound of bells continues to resonate far beyond the time when you can hear it, and the harmonics of special clearing bells made from seven metals resonate longer than ordinary ice-cream bells. When you use bells to purify a room, they leave its energy field crystal clear, instantly lifting feelings of weakness. If you are sensitive to the light spectrum of spaces, you will also feel a difference in the color spectrum of rooms, which have benefited from a sound-of-bells bath. This is because the sound of bells affects the vibrations of colors, slicing through their spectrums of light and bringing strength to the auras of colors that surround animate and inanimate objects.

Larger bells give off deeper sounds and smaller bells lighter ones. I recommend using smaller bells, which create a lighter, healthier energy level in a room. If you can afford it, get a silver or golden bell ito tap into the energy of the Moon and Sun. Even better, get Tibetan or Mongolian bells made from seven metals, as these offer multi-dimensional benefits that reflect the attributes of the seven planets. They create an aura of strength and good health. Brass bells also emit wonderful sounds, especially when a small amount of gold is added to them. When you ring bells in your living space, you will discover that their sounds grow clearer with every fresh ring; walk around each room three times clockwise, and feel your spirits lift. In no time at all, you feel energized.

Ringing bells and playing music shifts heavy energy and promotes and happier atmosphere.

When you feel misunderstood, clear the clutter behind your bed   138

Aggravation comes from being misunderstood. When your well-meaning statements and your well-intentioned actions are completely misread, you are left wondering why people seem to be having such a hard time appreciating your positive motivations. It will seem like luck is against you. There are few things more discouraging than having to accept being misunderstood on a regular basis. This seems to happen frequently to people who sleep with a lot of junk behind them. Look at what is behind your bed–even if the stuff there is not what you might ordinarily call "junk," at least move it to another place. To have your motives seen as positive and pure in all your work and social interactions, it is imperative to sleep with the space your head points to clear of junk. Look also at what is on the other side of the wall your head is pointing to. If what is on the other side is a toilet, it is

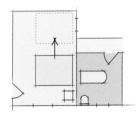

Protect Your Sleeping Space
Remove clutter under and around the bed; check if your bed shares a wall with a toilet, as this may negatively affect your space.

a good idea to move the bed so it is against another wall. Sharing a sleeping wall with a toilet or bath on the other side tends to create mixed signals in all of your words and actions.

It is the same if the other side of the wall has a staircase, a kitchen, or a storeroom filled with a lifetime's worth of clutter. Clear all the clutter behind your bed.

When you feel ugly, clear your closet   139

Physical beauty is a state of mind. Feeling unattractive is a very exhausting and discouraging illusion. For people who are well-schooled in the transformation of attitudes and positive visualization exercises, it is not so difficult to shake off feelings that make them feel insecure. But many people need help with transforming their mental states and support to clear out old clothes, past looks, and tired images. Systematically go through your closets and choose outfits to either give away or throw out. Get rid of anything and everything that makes you feel unattractive. First discard clothes that look old,

faded, and obviously from another season or era of fashion. Then remove clothes that no longer fit you or are no longer suitable for your lifestyle. Then throw away clothes that you simply dislike, for whatever reason. Each time you update your wardrobe, set yourself a goal to get rid of one-third of your clothes. This creates a vacuum for more flattering clothes to come to you. Your insecurities will evaporate in the light of your firm intentions to improve your appearance. Looking better leads to feeling better, and feeling better leads to your aura expanding into new realms for new experiences.

140 When you feel spaced out, do something different

in an activity of creating, building, or nurturing something. Turn your attention towards something or someone else other than yourself. This shift in attention and emphasis to another outside living thing or being, is an excellent way to restore your energy, and both pets and plants are excellent objects of refocusing your attention and awareness. They symbolize growth chi and when you are engaging in planting, for instance, you are, in effect, fostering "growth chi." It is the same as playing with your dog or feeding your fish.

A feeling of heaviness can sometimes make you feel "spaced out." This has you feeling unbalanced, as though the energy propelling you forward is somehow out of sync with the rest of the world. It is a malady that strikes when you are simply overloaded with too much work, when too many things seem to be going wrong, and there is just too much stress in your life. It can be the first stage of burn-out and is a sign to step back from whatever you are doing.

Taoists believe that keeping healthy fish helps cure tiredness because they bring in active yang energy.

Seeking balance

The best antidote for this feeling is to focus on something that will engage you in an altogether different dimension, so do something different. For this, you will need to rebalance the vibration that resonates in your auric field.

Take up a new hobby. Enroll for a course. Do some planting in your garden. Get involved

Getting focused with fish

Another way to attract growth chi into your living field is to bring fish into your life. Fish signify life in the realm of water. As a quick-fix, here is a Taoist secret. Taoists recommend keeping fish to de-stress the mind; it apparently makes tiredness evaporate. You should keep fish in the colors that correspond to your season of birth. If you were born in winter, keep black fish; in summer, keep red fish; in spring, keep green fish; and, in the fall, keep white fish. If you were born in the months just before or just after summer, keep yellow fish.

The Taoists go on to advise that if you are running your own business, keep some fish in your office according to the color of your wife's season of birth. If you are a woman, follow your own season of birth and, if you are a bachelor, the season of birth of your girlfriend. If you are a a single man, use your own season of birth color.

The life force of symbols–mystical and ordinary

141

Every spiritual and esoteric tradition has special symbols that seem to carry an intrinsic force for good. The Chinese believe that one can change the quality and movement of energy in any space simply by invoking the power of symbols. These symbols can be as simple as circles and squares, as ordinary as specially potent numbers, and as direct as special characters or words that symbolize something auspicious. They can also be celestial creatures that reflect the chi of other realms of the living world. Totems, divinities, gemstones, and mystical signs are also symbols whose power may be invoked.

The Chinese regard symbols as expressions of the five elements, which have either a yin or a yang manifestation. The concept of yin and yang also has its own symbol–the tai chi symbol. This symbol is a circle made up of a dark half and a light half. It signifies completeness. So when you draw a

Symbols of Fortune
The Pa Kua symbol and symbolic calligraphy (left); the simple symbolism of geometric shapes; and the yin yang, or tai chi, symbol.

Yin yang (tai chi) symbol

circle with your hands, you can be invoking the power of the tai chi symbol. When you fill it with a dark and a light side, you are accessing the two sides of wholeness–both the yin and the yang.

Symbols and the mind

Symbols focus and magnify thoughts. They also transmit messages of intentions and affirmations into the cosmic universal source. Some say this source is the sum of all worlds' consciousnesses, so that, in essence, it represents universal consciousness. This universal source of energy has the power to actualize all states of mind-awareness, knowing, and materializing. When invoked by a knowing mind, symbols take on a powerful resonance that instantly transcends the energy of the space we occupy. The key that unlocks the power of mystical symbols is the mind.

Amulets and Opportunities

I discovered the power of mystical symbols by chance, early in my corporate days, and since then my knowledge of symbols has expanded without me being consciously aware of it. Strangely, symbols seem to appear in my life first, usually as amulets I am asked to wear or carry "for my protection." Over the years, I have become increasingly conscious of "lucky breaks" related to the timing of benchmark opportunities that have come into my life at certain points, and of last-minute changes of schedule that brought new options to me. All the milestones of my life have been accompanied by symbolic amulets, gemstones, or talismans coming into my possession or into my home just prior to the event.

142 Symbols for power and protection

Symbols may be used to enhance living and working spaces, empower rooms, protect the mind, and expand consciousness with energy tapped directly from the universal divine source. The strategic placement of symbols and the deliberate wearing of them on your body will open the channel to this source of spiritual energy. Symbols are catalysts for revitalizing us in a way that transcends the merely material, although they are themselves often material. They can be made of different substances–metal, wood, or things taken from the earth.

When made of metal, symbols contain powerful energies present in the planetary system. They can be made of gold, silver, copper, brass, aluminum, steel, or combinations of these metals. Metals invoke the power of the Sun, the Moon, Jupiter, Venus, Mercury, Saturn, and Mars. These seven planets symbolize a range of aspirations, attributes, and strengths. Symbols made of metal are said to embody various kinds of good fortune, and different manifestations of courage.

This gold and silver jewelry displays the knot and buckle symbols.

Symbolic Jewelry

Symbols fashioned into jewelry are best made in gold–either yellow or white. When combined with diamonds, they are potentially the most powerful of symbols, because diamonds are the hardest of the earth symbols–the natural crystals of our world that have the exciting potential to unlock and manifest an enormous range of good fortune to those within its sphere of influence. Perhaps this is why the wearing of jewelry fashioned into auspicious symbols is something that has survived since prehistoric times. It is indeed very significant that all the Royal families and cosmic deities of almost every tradition of the world are described as being adorned with gemstones from head to toe.

Consecrating symbols

Symbols need not always be worn to be effective. Wherever they are, they create their own auras, which can usually be strengthened through spiritual consecrations. When symbols come alive through having been consecrated, they emit strong power indeed. Consecration rituals can be as simple as passing symbols over fragrant incense while mantras are chanted (in essence, secret sounds known to spiritual masters), or they can be complicated offering rituals done by holy men who happen to be around.

Totems

Symbols made of wood tend to be favored by more primitive societies. Symbols are often elaborately carved and hung at door entrances and inside houses, and are said to bring long life, blessings from deities, and a natural death. Totems are very popular among many hill peoples in Asia and Native American tribes. Rites of consecration are usually performed for totems, such as the ritualized dotting of the eyes of celestial dragons, or the symbolic taking off in flight of the phoenix that rises from the ashes.

A wooden dragon totem.

Activating energy by drawing symbols in the air · 143

The powers of symbols may be invoked in various ways. For instance, you can set specially made auspicious symbols of good fortune in the corners of your home to attract different kinds of luck.

Good fortune symbols

In recent years, interest in and demand for feng shui symbols of good fortune has grown. Increasing numbers of people are tuning into the mysterious way they seem to attract good fortune into the home, and so more people have them there. Some examples of these symbols are the three-legged toad, the dragon, the tortoise, bird feathers, and special coins. These are not mystical symbols. They are "good fortune" symbols recognized by the Chinese for centuries as catalysts of good luck. Now they are very nearly universally known. The dragon, for example, is today recognized and loved as a powerful symbol of good fortune, whereas, in the not-too-distant past, only the Chinese saw this celestial creature this way.

The three-legged toad is a symbol for wealth.

Mystic symbols

There are also simple mystical symbols which feature in many traditions. These can be invoked by drawing their shapes in the air while using incense to cleanse a room's auric layers. Opposite are a few techniques for evoking simple symbols. The process described is the Taoist method of invocation.

How to Draw Symbols

1. Close your right hand into a fist. Extend the index and middle fingers, letting them point straight ahead. Your thumb will naturally hold the other two fingers, so your hand is a gun shape. Practice drawing a circle with the two extended fingers. Learn to draw the following symbols to invoke their powers. Do it several times as you move around the room.

2. Draw a complete circle in the empty space in front of you to invoke the unity of family or employees, or the successful completion of a project. The circle has a multitude of excellent symbolic definitions and is very powerful. It signifies the Sun, the Moon, the cycles of life, and the concept of fullness and wholeness. If you feel that your life lacks meaning, or your family seems disunited, invoke closer ties by summoning the power of the circle. Draw the circle, moving your fingers in a clockwise direction in order to generate its vibrations. When you want to use the circle for healing purposes, draw the circle in an anti-clockwise direction. End the drawing session with a zigzag movement of the hand and fingers in a downward gesture; this signals the completion of the ritual.

3. Draw a square to signify protection and to create a state of prosperity and abundance. Think of the four corners of the room you occupy and mentally connect these corners as you trace a square with your outstretched fingers. Begin from the top corner and draw the square in a clockwise direction for protection and to attract prosperity vibrations. Again, end the session with a zigzag movement of the hand and fingers in a downward gesture to signal completion of the ritual.

4. Draw a cross at the entrance of your home to signify an invisible talisman protecting it. Draw the horizontal line before drawing the vertical line. Do this three times to set up an invisible force field of protective energy.

144 Yantra symbols are powerful protectors

Hindus invoke the powerful symbols they call yantras for protection and various kinds of specific "good fortune luck." Yantras comprise several triangles, one on top of the other, and these are usually cast as images on large gold coins. The gold usually has the utmost purity. When you visit India, it is a good idea to look for these yantra coins, which usually come as jewelry featuring one of the Indian goddesses of wealth, knowledge, wisdom, or love. Merely having such a yantra medallion in the home creates an auric field around it so that it is protected from negative energies, it is said. There are also planetary yantras, which signify special protections for different days of the week.

The Louvre Pyramid, Paris, France, has strong yin energy that is appropriate for a museum.

Many spiritual traditions regard the triangle as a powerful symbol because it represents the trinity of heaven, earth, and mankind. The triangle also represents the pyramid, which is itself a powerful symbol of preservation. The pyramid is a three-dimensional version of the triangle or Holy Trinity, which can symbolize the family unit as well as the time dimensions of past, present, and future.

Yantra designs evoke powerful trinities that underpin many spiritual traditions, such as heaven, earth, and mankind.

A triangle ritual

A powerful Taoist amulet ritual utilizes the triangle symbol. Taoists believe that, when you bury three small crystals (crystal balls or natural single-pointed crystals) in the garden or driveway in front of your main door, positioning them in the form of a triangle with the point facing outward, it is the best possible protection for your house. The energy they create taps into the ground's energy so that it is self-rejuvenating and self-replenishing.

When to avoid the pyramind

Do not place the pyramid symbol inside your home, or on your desk or, worse, live or work in a building that has a pyramid roof line. Pyramids tend to attract and store yin chi and are excellent in the design of yin dwellings, such as tombs. The Louvre Pyramid, in Paris is fine because it is a museum, and its glass structure also feeds light into the corridors that lead to its heart. In the home, however, the pyramid is too powerful a yin symbol. Even for offices and large shopping complexes, the pyramid can be a dangerous symbol and is best avoided.

The symbol of the Lo Shu square—the sigil 145

Another powerful symbol that is highly respected by masters of the esoteric is that of the Lo Shu numbers. It also appears in other traditions. In Indian Vedic astrology, the symbol is referred to as the sigil. A range of forms of planetary numerology about lucky numbers is derived from the sigil that is both intriguing and complex.

A simpler way of tapping into mystical codes is to activate the sign of the sigil. Trace the nine numbers in an ascending order around the nine-grid square illustrated here, and you will derive the sign of the sigil. (Look at the illustration below, which shows how the sigil is formed.) The sign of the sigil is known as the Nine Emperor Sign in Chinese folklore. Using and invoking the sign of the sigil is supposedly one of the secrets of Taoist feng shui; it is said to be the sign to invoke if you want to overcome the negative influence of bad luck numbers flying into your home or office space.

The sigil ritual

Stand outside your home and draw the sign of the sigil as indicated in the illustration. You will see that the numbers are placed where they are according to the Lo Shu square shown here.

Use the hand mudra for invoking mystic symbols (the index and middle fingers point horizontally outwards with the thumb holding down the other two fingers) to draw the sign of the sigil. First, settle your mind, then mentally state your motivation before drawing the sign of the sigil about one foot (30 cm) in front of you, three times. Then quickly draw the zigzag sign before you in order to complete the ritual.

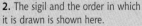

Use the hand mudra for evoking mystic symbols.

This ritual of invoking the sigil at a house entrance is said to release the flow of good chi into a house, thereby overcoming any bad luck, illness, or potential loss.

The Lo Shu and Sigil

1. The Lo Shu Square is one of the most important anchor symbols in the practice of "compass formula feng shui." It is called the Lo Shu square because it is said to have been brought to the legendary Emperor Fu Hsi on the back of a tortoise who floated up along the River Lo in China. The arrangement of the numbers 1 to 9 in the nine-grid square is said to be mystically powerful, and any three of the numbers equal a sum of 15, whether added vertically, horizontally, or diagonally. The number 15 is significant, because this is the number of days it takes a waxing moon to become a full

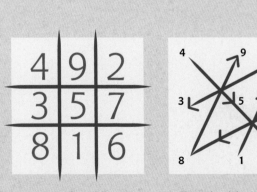

moon, and a waning moon to become a new moon. So the Lo Shu square symbolizes the influence of time on the affairs of mankind.

2. The sigil and the order in which it is drawn is shown here.

146 Numerology and lucky Lunar Year numbers

The numbers 1 to 9 hold important cyclical significance for the Chinese. Numbers are said to have different strengths during different cyclical periods for different people and different houses.

Numerology, or the science of numbers, exerts significant influences on the practice of Flying Star Feng Shui—one of the most powerful formulas in feng shui practice that uses a compass. In it, there are lucky and unlucky numbers, strong and weak numbers. The feng shui master who knows how to read a feng shui chart will be able to predict good and bad events that will happen to the residents of a house just by looking at the numbers, and the combinations of numbers, indicated for different rooms. Advanced feng shui in the hands of an experienced feng shui master can thus assist people to avoid misfortunes, illnesses, and accidents.

It is also possible to calculate your lucky number(s) based on your birth date. Numbers that bring luck to the spaces you occupy are based on the Kua formula. This is determined by a simple calculation using your Lunar Year of birth.

How to Calculate Your Kua Number

Take the last two numbers of your Lunar Year of birth. You will need to check whether you were born before or after the Lunar New Year in your year of birth. Usually if you were born after the middle of February, there is no need to make any adjustment, since after that the Lunar Year coincides with the western year. Really only those born before mid-February need to check when the lunar New Year started in their year of birth.

1. Add the last two numbers in your year of birth until you reduce them to a single digit.

2a. Women should add 5 to the result and add again, if necessary, to obtain a single digit. That number (between 1 to 9) is your Kua number—your lucky number. For women born after 2000, add 6.

   For example, if the year of birth is 1959, 5 + 9 = 14, then 1 + 4 = 5.
   Then add 5, so 5 + 5 = 10, 1 + 0 = 1.

2b. Men should subtract 10; the resulting number will be their Kua number, i.e., their lucky number. Men born after 2000 should subtract 9.

Examples:
For a woman born on August 6, 1949:
Add 4+9=13 and then 1+3=4 and then 4+5 = 9, so the woman's Kua number is 9.

For a man born on January 3, 1939:
To adjust for the Lunar New Year, subtract one year, and use 1938 as the year of his birth.
Add 3+8=11 and then 1+1=2 and then 10-2 = 8, so the man's Kua number is 8.

Once you have your Kua number, you can identify numbers that are said to be good for you and ones that are supposed to be bad for you. This is because the numbers 1 to 9 are divided into two groups:

East group numbers are	**West** group numbers are
1, 3, 4, and **9.**	**2, 5, 6, 7,** and **8.**

All the numbers in the same group are lucky. All the numbers in the other group are unlucky for your group. Try to use your lucky numbers as often as possible.

The special power of Ho Tu numbers 147

In Chinese tradition, there is a set of numbers known as the Ho Tu, which are number combinations thought to be very lucky. These were brought on the back of a mythical dragon-horse, known as the unicorn, or Chi Lin, and the numbers are said to indicate different kinds of good fortune.

Ho Tu numbers and house numbers
Ho Tu numbers are said to be extremely lucky when they are in their waxing cycle or at their height, and very unlucky when they are in their waning cycle. Whether they are waxing or waning depends on the direction your house faces.

6 and 1 bring excellent "education luck" when the cycle is waxing and the house faces East or Southeast. If your address is 16 or 61, the children in your house will be very intelligent and talented, and they will bring honor to your family. This combination is at its height in the North. But this combination brings bad luck and accidents to the patriarch when the house faces South. In this direction the numbers 6 and 1 wane, bringing negative influences.

2 and 7 bring financial luck to a house facing Southwest or Northeast. In the South, they are also lucky. But if the house faces Northwest or West, there could be illnesses and accidents in it.

3 and 8 will bring success in politics and "descendants luck" to a house facing South, East, and Southeast, but harm to children when it faces Southwest.

4 and 9 bring excellent business luck to a house facing North, West, and Northwest.

Bad or good symbolism of house numbers depends upon the direction in which your home faces.

Ho Tu Number Combinations

1 and 6   2 and 7   3 and 8   4 and 9

But when it faces East and has an address that incorporates the numbers 4 and 9, extreme bad luck is brought to the people occupying the house.

The special power of these Ho Tu number combinations is usually felt when the house address incorporates the particular combination of numbers. If yours is a lucky orientation, sit back and enjoy the good fortune. But if your address has these numbers and your house is facing the waning direction, the way to overcome any negative impact these numbers have is simply to use words instead of numbers on your house address; that way, the symbolism will be immediately dispelled.

148 Identifying lucky numbers with your birth date

There is another way to identify numbers that are lucky for you. It is based on the day of your date of birth. If you were born on June 17, then the number $1+7=8$ is said to be lucky for you. When this number is the number of the floor level of your office, room, road, or precinct, or if it features in your address or zip code–it will bring you good luck. Note that this method uses only your day number reduced to a single digit.

You can find your lucky numbers using ancient Chinese formulas.

A second method uses the more broad-based range of numbers signified by your full date of birth. For instance, if you were born on June 6, 1977, then the numbers 661977 would bring you good luck. Any of these numbers bring you good luck if they are somewhere in your address. You can also reduce these numbers to a single digit by adding them together. Based on this method, your lucky number would then be

$6+6+1+9+7+7=36$ and then $3+6=9$, so 9 is your birth number and is lucky for you. When you start to become conscious of the influence of your lucky numbers on your well-being in this way, you will find yourself being persuaded to believe in their symbolism. You will find that there really are days when you feel better than other days, that there are days when better things happen to you than other days.

The number three is a favorite lucky number. It represents creativity, the sum of the energy of the numbers 1 and 2.

It is possible to go more deeply into the study of numerology than this, however. Almost all cultural traditions, irrespective of religion, have their different methods for calculating lucky numbers, and it is good to use the method with which you feel most comfortable.

I have used my day of birth and my Kua number to determine my lucky number for the past thirty years and, I have to say, these numbers have rarely failed me–even on the roulette table!

Finding Your Lucky Number

Most of us have a few lucky numbers, not just a single lucky number. You will discover that once you have identified a few of your relevant lucky numbers, you will begin to note lucky things that happen to you that are associated with your auspicious numbers. For instance, if you were born on the April 11, 1949, then you will begin to see that the number 11, which reduces to 2, is lucky for you. In addition, you can also find out what your birth number is based on by adding all of your birth numbers: $1+1+4+1+9+4+9=29$. In this case, the numbers are further added together as $2+9$, which is 11.

These numbers add up to 11 and then to 2. So, in this instance, you may be very sure that the numbers 11 reduced to 2 will be extremely lucky for you. If you incorporate these numbers into your house somehow, you will benefit from them as lucky numbers. Find a house address that has your lucky numbers in it. Get telephone numbers that contain them also.

Attracting good energy with the sun symbol 149

Another way to benefit your home is to invoke the sun with this powerful symbol that combines the sun's rays with the eight directions of the compass. This mystical symbol features in many advanced ancient systems that utilize a visualized light source for healing work.

Study the symbol shown here carefully. Note the sequence in which it is drawn. Note the direction of the strokes. Use your fingers to draw this symbol in the rooms of your home that need a dose of sun energy. As you draw it, imagine that you are creating a ball of brilliant bright light. Then visualize the sun's brilliant rays emanating outward from it and washing your rooms with powerful light energy. This is a very potent mystical symbol that requires a simple visualization. It sends light rays into your living space. Do remember to complete the ritual with the zigzag hand movement.

When to use the sun symbol

A good time to use this is when someone in your house is ill, or having a long period of bad luck in terms of opportunities drying up or losing a job. It strengthens and revitalizes the energy present, and improves things for those who are suffering. For someone who is very ill, imagine tapping into the light source of the sun and bringing the light into the room occupied by the sick person. This symbol has the power to create additional energy that will help anyone feel better.

As you invoke mystical symbols to call upon the universal source of energy, it is really helpful to generate the motivation of selfless compassion within yourself. Think positive thoughts as you perform this ritual. Mystical symbols always work best when your thoughts and intentions are good. The more unconditional and altruistic the energy of love that is used to empower the invoking of a particular symbol, then the more powerful it will be.

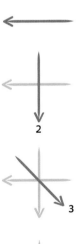

The sun symbol can be used for powerful healing and energizing. Draw it in the air, following the sequence illustrated below. It can also be displayed in art, or here, as part of a mirror design, to attract positive yang energy into a room.

150 Activating the mysterious power of the infinity symbol

Perhaps one of the most powerful symbols I have ever come across is the infinity symbol–which looks like an elongated number eight laid on its side. This symbol instantly lifts the energy of any space. If you use your index and middle fingers to draw the infinity sign as you walk around each room of your home, you will almost immediately feel a positive difference in its overall energy.

The ritual

Simply walk around the house in a clockwise direction and use your hands to draw the symbol in large elongated arcs in front of you. As you do this, visualize powerful beams of light emanating from the symbol and bathing your home with a powerful glow. The infinity sign has amazing healing and protective qualities. Inhabitants' moods are said to immediately soften, and anger is transformed into patience and tolerance. The next time someone yells and screams in your house, quickly tune into the space and, in your mind, mentally draw the symbol several times in the air. Note how long it takes for the upset person's mood to soften.

Try it also when someone is ill. Draw the infinity sign in the room where the sick person is sleeping–walk three times around the room in a clockwise direction and let the sign work its powerful magic. In addition to regularly invok-

Display the infinity or number eight symbol on soft furnishings or in decorative art to keep up the good atmosphere in a room.

Evoking the infinity sign using the index and middle fingers immediately lifts the energy in a room, clearing away residual negativities.

ing the infinity sign, I also have a wonderful figure of eight made of solid crystal and filled with flecks of real 24-carat gold dust inside. The figure eight is itself regarded as a powerfully auspicious symbol and of course it is the infinity symbol placed upright. I feel its benevolent glow in my home all the time as it sends out auspicious chi.

Drawing the symbol on paper

You can also have this symbol carved onto furniture, or simply draw it on paper and burn it, in order to activate its powerful magic. Doing so will activate the mysterious power of the infinity symbol. If you physically "draw" this sign in the space in front of you using your hand, always remember to use the completion mudra (the zigzag) to seal in its benefits.

Creating personal symbols   151

There are many different symbols we can invoke to improve the sense of sanctuary and comfort of a living space. Keeping homes clean and filled with vitality through the different realms of our consciousness often require us to raise our awareness of the different realms of chi in our environment. Only then can we enjoy the good things of the material world and also find inner happiness that transcends time and space.

In the world of mind, body, and spirit, we can choose a host of transcendental allies who may become our personal bodyguards and protectors. These might be from the animal or bird world. We also can choose symbols from deep within the earth—stones of every shape, size or color—or objects from the ocean depths: pearls, seashells, seaweeds, or exotic fish. The creation of personal symbols is not unlike the making of personal amulets and talismans.

Symbols that are public rather than personal become business insignias or brands that express a company's values.

How Crystals Became Me

When you practice focusing your consciousness to empower objects and symbols, they gain strength simply because you imbue them with strength. I first suspected this to be so when I was in my twenties. I had always had an affinity with natural crystals, so in the Seventies when I first became aware that I could not resist the few single-pointed crystals that came my way, I went along with my instincts and indulged myself with them. From then on, crystals just kept coming to me. People would make me the most stunning gifts of single and double-pointed crystals, and I would find crystal clusters being mailed to me all the time.

I always cleansed and empowered them. For this, I used fragrance and incense and, when I chanted mantras and did my meditations, they would always be nearby.

My collection has since expanded into crystal balls purchased from all over the world and crystal malas (i.e., beads strung into Buddhist rosaries comprising 108 beads). And, of course, I am also a great believer in wearing colored precious stones set with gold and diamonds. Every piece of crystal I own today brings me wonderful feelings of security and well-being. I feel revitalized each time I stroke and hold my crystals.

In short, they have become my personal symbols.

152 In the living room, utilize the harmonious mystical knot

Displaying the mystical knot in the living room warms up your relationships.

If you want to create a powerful ambience of harmony and friendship within your home, keep your living room well-energized and activated. Never allow it to become cluttered with things lying all over the place. Also introduce auspicious symbols there that will activate the good energy within it.

Perhaps the most beneficial symbol to activate in the living room is the mystical knot. This is the knot of endless love, which lovers can wear for great benefit and harmony. The knot is eternal, never ending, with no beginning and no end. The mystical knot is exactly like the infinity symbol, only it is the infinity symbol multiplied and magnified. You can draw the symbol into your space and use incense to consecrate its invisible presence. However, you can also acquire material mystical knots in the form of jade hangings that are tied with red string, which empowers them. Hang mystical knots at each of the four corners of your living room. Hang them a little high up the wall. Not only will your family life improve and relationships between its members become more loving, but your social lives will also become warmer and more meaningful. You can also draw this symbol on paper and keep it folded in your wallet, although it is really at its most powerful when fashioned from gold.

153 Improving relationships with brass mirrors

An empowered brass mirror is magical for giving all of your relationships a boost. These may be relationships with loved ones, friends, employers and employees, bosses and colleagues, siblings, parents, or children. They are also excellent for absorbing feelings of enmity and envy from others that are directed at you. A side benefit is that it also diffuses potential problems and politicking that may be directed at you without your knowledge.

The brass mirror I am suggesting is a small mirror about three inches in diameter that has two reflective surfaces. It is perhaps one of the most effective feng shui tools for guarding your livelihood from being spoiled

Brass mirrors protect you by absorbing negative feelings from other people.

by troublemakers. In the days of emperors, many Chinese court officials used it. For many centuries, its importance as a tool for overcoming bad luck has been a very well-kept secret guarded by master practitioners, especially those skilled in Taoist inner feng shui practices.

In the bedroom, place a brass mirror that has been exposed to moonlight (and so empowered by the moon) so that it faces the bedroom door. This ensures a good night's sleep. In the living room, place it on a side table, facing the main door. In the office, place it behind you on your right side. Brass mirrors in the office protect you from being negatively affected by gossip, politicking, and troublemakers.

In the dining room, activate the harvest sign   154

It is always a good idea to maintain a clutter-free environment in the dining room, since this is where the good fortune of the house manifests on a daily basis in the form of food on the table. Here good fortune is expressed regularly and in tune with the needs of the family. So the dining room should always be viewed as the heart of the home, a place which must be kept clean and full of vitality—a veritable storehouse of good chi. In many homes, insufficient attention is focused on keeping this room energized. It should have sufficient light, be able to benefit from the soft breezes of the outdoors and feel spacious and bright. Try eating in cramped spaces and you will feel the difference. Feeling cramped is different from being cozy.

In the dining room, symbols that depict harvesting, which signifies the successful reaping of one's hard work and effort, creates an ambience of plenty. So hang a painting there of freshly picked fruit, or a picture of farmers bringing in the corn or wheat from the fields. Pictures of harvesting, or of miles and miles of fields that are ripe with corn, rice, or millet, are powerful symbols of abundance and, when placed in a dining room, they suggest that the family eating there will never lack good fortune. There will always be plenty of food on the table.

Harvest symbols include corn sheaves, corn dollies, fresh fruit bowls or baskets, and paintings or other artifacts depicting actual harvesting in fields or a general abundance of food.

Dining rooms of the home always benefit a home's residents when they are decorated with symbols of abundance. If possible, you can even install a wall mirror there, which effectively doubles the food on the table.

Do note that this is quite different from placing mirrors in the kitchen. Mirrors in the kitchen bring bad luck and often make accidents happen. But mirrors in the dining room, especially when they reflect signs of harvesting, food, and abundance, are very good luck. Mirrors that reflect open fields, rivers, a lake, or just the blue sky, are very auspicious indeed. Invest in a single low cabinet to ensure that this room is always kept free of junk and clutter, and dine as elegantly and in as much comfort as you can. This is the secret of success.

155   In all the bedrooms, invoke moon energy

Moon energy is yin energy, but it is a restful kind of yin energy that is benevolent and full of mystical chi–the kind that resonates positively and promotes the subconscious growth of the spirit. Many Taoist rituals connected with the art of chi kung, which engage the human body's meridians and auric layers, draw on chi from the moon. Experts in chi kung are usually also well-schooled in the practice of absorbing light energy from the moon; to do this successfully requires some practice under a well-qualified Master.

To create a cozy and restful ambience in your bedroom, evoke moon energy using mirrors and crystals.

Mirrors and moon energy

Moon energy can also be symbolically gathered by using auspicious mirrors. When you shine a circular mirror at a brightly lit full moon, it is said to be able to absorb a great deal of moon energy. If you stand facing the moon and visualize the light of the moon permeating your aura as you

Empower crystals and mirrors with full moon energy, then place them beside a bed, facing the bedroom's entrance door.

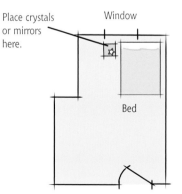

Place crystals or mirrors here.

Window

Bed

rhythmically breathe in and out, you will also absorb some powerful moon chi.

The key is to absorb good moon energy, i.e., the light of the moon during auspicious occasions and lucky days. The Chinese love the full moon that occurs on the fifteenth day of the Lunar New Year or during the harvest festival of mid-fall. If you forget to tap into moon energy during the auspicious full moon days, or if the weather makes clouds hide the light of the moon, then the next best thing is to wait for the waxing moon, the moon that gradually grows brighter. The light from the waxing moon is always auspicious and lucky, while the light from a waning moon signifies weak energy that is becoming weaker by the day.

Activating "three-generation luck" in a family room 156

One of the most special of auspicious objects you can place in your family living or dining room is an image showing at least three generations of your family looking happy, abundant, and prosperous. Family portraits represent an excellent display of family good fortune. Those that include three generations–the grandfather, father, and sons–are said to be the most auspicious. The three generations can be featured as being all-male or include the women of the family as well.

In my home, I have "three-generation luck" symbols in my living and dining rooms, as I am a great believer in family harmony and family prosperity. I, my mother, and my daughter, represent the three generations of my family. My mother is still a healthy lady of nearly eighty years old.

My husband's mother and father have long since passed away. In order to balance our portrait with male energy, I also display three generations of emperors as porcelain figurines. This is placed in the living room.

When you activate with three-generation luck, you are generating the chi of continuity–continuity of prosperity and good health, and plenty of descendants' luck. The Chinese have always been a very pragmatic race of people. They know that these are people's three major aspirations that lead to fulfillment and happiness. The Chinese regard all other ills as being fabrications of the mind. So symbols for the continuity of a family's good fortune should always be present in its home. This invites true harmony and balance into family members' lives.

Empower your home with the longevity symbol 157

The Chinese regard the longevity symbol as the ultimate amulet. It is very easy to find and identify simply because it is present on so many things made in China–decorative pieces made of porcelain and jade, vases, furniture, jewelry, and clothing. It is on many silk robes purchased in Chinese art emporiums and was present on all the imperial robes worn by the Chinese Emperor and the members of his family. If you happen to own a figurine of the auspicious God of longevity–an old man with a long balding forehead who carries a peach and a long staff–you will see that the robe he wears carries the longevity symbol.

There are many modern versions of this symbol, which not only symbolizes long life but also acts as a protection against unnatural death, accidents, murder, burglary, terrorism, and so forth. When you empower your home and your body with the longevity symbol, it creates energy for good health and long life with a natural death. So do consider having it in your home.

The longevity symbol can be used as a decorative motif, or worn as jewelry,

158 Empowerments from trees

In recent years, many Taoist rituals for attuning to the valuable chi of the living fauna and flora that make up this planet have been revealed, as more masters decide to show their secrets to the world. One of the most wonderful ways of tuning into the chi of a city, or an area, is to identify the oldest tree in a park or neighborhood and become one with its chi. Always look for a healthy tree whose branches send out broad, thick leaves. The larger its leaves and the thicker its trunk is, the more generous the tree is. Look for a tree that stands in a strategic place where it can see many things and is surrounded regularly by many people. Such a tree possesses great wisdom.

Meditating with trees

Linking yourself with a tree's chi is very simple if you are accustomed to meditating regularly. Stand in front of it for a few minutes, allowing it to become aware of and get to know you. You might sit under the tree for a picnic before doing this. After a while, you will feel whether there is any affinity between you. When good vibrations exist between you and the tree, you will feel that it is the most natural thing in the world to place your palms flat against its trunk. Some people will experience an immediate surge of energy from doing this; others will need a little time. Close your eyes lightly and tune into the massive wisdom of the tree.

Tree energy is very sturdy. They have a life of their own and can procreate as well. In Chinese, tree chi is known as sheng chi or growth chi. The essence of tree energy is always growth energy, because wood is the only one of the five elements that grows. Of the five different types of chi–symbolized by the five elements: water, fire, metal, earth, and wood–it is the wood energy that you find in trees. Wood energy is excellent for fire people or people who need the warmth of the fire element, because wood energy produces fire energy.

Tree Energy for Fame

If you need recognition or success in your work, examinations, or any project in which you are involved, and you are feeling frustrated or disheartened, take a walk in a park or forest around the wood energy of powerful old trees.

Channeling earth energy from the roots of great trees 159

If you need the grounding energy of earth, you can probably use some help from these old trees. Think of the root system of these great trees burrowing deep into the ground, sending thousands of little roots in all directions. You can visualize earth chi being channeled from the land through this powerful root network.

Remember that not all ground has the same history or provenance, and certainly not all countries are alike. As someone who comes from Malaysia, for many years a developing country, I really looked forward very much to tuning into the "wealth" chi in the parks of prosperous cities like London and New York, and states like California.

I always enjoyed channeling earth energy from the trees I encountered in the redwood forests of Northern California and the pine trees in Colorado, where I spent many happy seasons skiing on the slopes of the Vale and surrounding ski areas. Usually it would take only a few minutes and it always seemed that I got a boost of strength and courage each time I hugged a tree tightly and visualized earth chi filling my body. Choose a healthy looking tree, perhaps the biggest tree in the park, and give it a hug.

Earth chi for courage

Earth chi is very grounding. It gives you courage and strength, and is like having an energy boost. It is free and has no side effects. This is the great priceless value of many of the ancient Taoists secret practices—they require no props to perform, only your body and your knowledge. This is why the possession of knowledge is so precious, for once you know how to borrow some strength, vitality, and courage from nature, you will be able to tap into a vast store-house of health and wealth-bringing chi. Always remember that, to absorb new energy, your mind must be uncluttered and simple.

However, always give back as much as you get, for it is this that keeps the chi flowing.

The roots of trees channel earth energy.

160 Spiritual cleansing with the cleaning mantra

There is a very special mantra which was given to me by my very precious guru, who is one of the highest of high lamas but whose humility is legend. His name is Lama Zopa Rinpoche, and his title is Kyabje, which means Lord of Refuge. I call him by the honorific Rinpoche, which means "precious one" in Tibetan. This is also the honorific by which the officially recognized reincarnated lamas in the Tibetan Buddhist traditions are known. It is a term of respect, but also of affection, which students accord their revered teachers.

In the course of my work with feng shui, I was most fortunate to meet Rinpoche. Over the past five years, Rinpoche has greatly encouraged me to continue with what I am doing, and his advice has been truly beneficial. Rinpoche has unwaveringly advised me to use feng shui to do as much good as possible, in order to ease the burdens of people's lives. His advice has

always been to generate the correct motivation, which is compassion for all suffering beings, and it is in this spirit and context that I am thrilled to be able to pass on this very simple cleansing mantra. It is only two words. As you sweep, clean, vacuum, and wipe the surfaces of your home, silently repeat this cleaning mantra over and over again in your mind.

Engaging your mind this way as you cleanse your dwelling space will add a spiritual dimension to the physical act of cleaning. It transmutes a simple, mundane domestic chore into Dharma (a Sanskrit word used by Hindus and Tibetans, which may be loosely defined as virtue, moral behavior, or work "of" or "in" truth) because, as you clean and chant, you visualize sweeping out all the negative things that may be present. Spiritual cleansing sweeps away not only physical dirt, but also all of the intangibles of negative karma that everyone carries and constantly creates.

After doing this simple activity every day for a year, observe how powerful your spiritual practice has been. Your home will be cleansed of all negative thoughts and attitudes, filled with spiritual vitality. Imagine how smooth the flow of life can become when all blockages are cleared.

Spiritual cleansing is physical and mental. Incense purifies on both these levels, so it is good to burn it after a clear out.

The Cleaning Mantra
Durupang, Timapang

As you clean or sweep, repeating this mantra to yourself, think: "This sweeps away all defilements, negative thoughts, and obstacles in our lives that block us from awakening to the true nature of all things. This also dissolves all the anger, attachment, and ignorance in our minds."

Creating a home altar to open pathways into spirituality   161

It does not matter what faith you follow. If you want to open pathways that lead to growth in awareness of all things spiritual, you might wish to consider setting up a small altar in your home. Altars express spiritual aspirations, and the best kind of altars are those dedicated to the God presence with which we each are most familiar and comfortable. I am one of those who believes that God is a word that signifies and personifies the highest good in us.

I have many altars in my home and they create a wonderful spiritual river of energy that is really very beautiful. When unhappiness arises in the house, it evaporates pretty quickly. When there is anger, it also dissipates in no time at all, and when those of us in the house suffer from fear, dissatisfaction, or frustration, something always happens to distract us from our negative emotions.

My altars are rather elaborate, with plenty of the five offering objects that are usually associated with altars: flowers, water, food, incense, and lights. I have been taught to replace these offerings daily in order to invoke the spiritual presence of cosmic forces that bless my home and engender within us all the desire to live virtuous lives and be beneficial to others. Virtue in this instance does not mean being goody-two-shoes, but rather that

we observe the basic tenets of not harming others and not doing anything in excess.

You can set up your altar according to what works for you. I have often been asked if altars need to be consecrated, and I would say preferably so. But, here again, it is up to you really. What I am advocating is the notion that, by inviting the God presence into your home, you create a spiritual energy that can only do you good.

Altars do not have to be traditional; exhibiting eclectic items you love can be uplifting.

162 Display a crystal obelisk empowered with mantras

Another excellent spiritual practice, which I picked up from associating with the monks and nuns of various monasteries I have visited and continue to visit, is the immensely powerful spiritual cleansing of space that takes place when we display holy mantras in our homes. However, this is not a habit confined only to Buddhists.

All believers of spiritual traditions seem to like displaying prayers and religious sayings. For instance, I have been in Christian homes that have the most beautiful spiritual energy because on the walls are holy scriptures or the words of Jesus Christ on them. I have also been in Muslim homes that feel incredibly peaceful, then I'll notice, hanging above doorways and in rooms, beautifully scripted words from the holy Koran. What I have observed is that the impact of these spiritual sayings is wonderfully magnified when feng shui is combined with them.

Mantras and crystals

One way of magnifying the powerful energy of mantras and holy scriptures is to write them on natural crystals. Since the obelisk is one of the most spiritually powerful shapes in existence, I find that writing a mantra on a crystal obelisk and then displaying it in a living room, with a bright light shining on it, instantly changes the energy of a room. I recommend the obelisk because of its special

The mantra Om Mani Padme Hum (below) and, above right, a crystal inscribed with a sacred mantra in gold.

magnifying power. Symbols emanate vibrations which, when transmitted, permeate and empower rooms with their special properties. The obelisk shape is especially empowering. If you doubt its power, turn your mind to the obelisk symbols in Washington, London, Paris, and other cities.

You can also use a natural single-pointed crystal, or a crystal ball, but the obelisk works fastest of all. You may want to write the powerful holy words "Om Ah Hum" on your crystal. Having these three words in your home signifies that all things and objects inside it are blessed with a spiritual essence of the highest good. Or you could use the powerful mantra Om Mani Padme Hum – "Hail O jewel in the lotus" – which is a mantra to the Buddha of Compassion. Use a gold ink pen for this.

ॐ मणि पद्मे हूँ

A special fire ritual to cleanse the spiritual essence of the home

163

This special fire ritual is a powerfully symbolic gesture, which you can do for the spiritual cleansing of your home at the end of each year. Choose a quiet corner of your garden that is large enough for you to start a small fire in it. You will need a stool on which you can sit while performing the ritual. You also will need some charcoal, dried pieces of wood, oil, and symbolic items signifying things you want to let go of.

In visualizations, scorpions, snakes and frogs can represent negativities that leave the body as the mind becomes purified.

The Fire-cleansing Ritual

Consider all the negative things in your life that you want to discard, all the grudges you may be holding, all the grief still locked up within you. The fire ritual burns away the things that make you unhappy. You can simply write down all the things that aggravate, frustrate, and annoy you–all the things that happened during the past year that you really want to release yourself from, things that went wrong and experiences you don't want to repeat. The fire burns away all of your problems and unhappiness, so write these down and put them aside to be burned.

Next, buy some black mustard seeds and black sesame seeds–these represent all the bad things and angry words that you said, and gossip that you passed on, which caused others to suffer. These will enable you to purify yourself of all the things you did during the year which offended or caused someone grief or unhappiness. Lay these aside to throw into the fire as well.

Finally, draw a small black scorpion, a small black snake, and a small black frog on a piece of paper. These represent all politicking, idle talk or gossip, and harmful or malicious intentions sent your way. Cut out the drawings and set them aside. These also are going to be consumed by the fire.

Now dig a hole in the corner of the garden that you have selected for the fire. The best time to do this fire puja is during the evening hours between 5 and 7 pm. Draw the infinity symbol on a piece of paper and place this flat on the ground in the hole. Stack some charcoal on top of the paper and start a fire. Then place some dried wood on top. Try to make the fire burn strongly in a small area. When you are satisfied that the fire is burning steadily, sit down in front of it and contemplate all the things you will be putting into the fire. First put in your drawings of the scorpion, the snake, and the frog; as these burn, imagine that all the desecrations and harm to your spirit caused by others gossiping about and creating difficulties for you are dissolved, cleansed, and purified.

Throw in the paper on which you wrote about people, events, and things that offended, upset, and annoyed you. As you watch the fire consume the paper, let go of all of those negative emotions and feelings and allow yourself to feel that you

are completely liberated from them. If you feel afraid, think that the fire also consumes all of your fears. With this ritual, you can be as egocentric as you wish. Do not allow the fire to burn out until you have finished the ritual. Add fuel to it as required.

Now pick up the black sesame and mustard seeds. Imagine that they represent all of your bad thoughts, harmful actions, and evil intentions. As the seeds burn, think that these negative aspects of yourself and those around you are cleansed, dissolved, and purified. This is the most important part of the ritual because it is really important to cleanse your environment of all of your and others' negative thoughts and actions–whether committed willingly or inadvertently. As you feed the seeds into the fire, let yourself experience a sense of remorse and regret about having caused anyone harm or grief. Make sure you burn all of the seeds that you bought. Do not leave anything behind.

When you have finished, allow the fire to burn out and then close the hole. Think that the earth has consumed all negative things. The idea behind this ritual is to make you feel purified and that your surroundings are purified.

164 Invoking the four protector-guardians for your home

There are four symbolic guardians that the Chinese are extremely fond of putting inside their homes. They are known as the four Heavenly Kings in Chinese legends, and as the four Dharma Protectors in Tibetan Buddhist stories. These guardians absorb the temptations and harm from spirits that come from the four directions. So, having them in your home keeps away damage caused by spirits and entities from other dimensions that cause illness, accidents, and injury to residents.

How the four protectors help

The four heavenly guardians protect us from the harm we may inflict upon ourselves, which is usually the result of our non-virtuous actions such as killing, stealing, and acting dishonorably or in an evil manner. This is why they are referred to as dharma protectors. They protect us from the evil and negative parts of ourselves. These four guardians hold a symbolic tool unique to their activities, and they each take charge of a different compass direction.

The guardian of the East: Mo Li Ching holds a magic sword with the words "earth, water, fire, and wind" on its blade. His sword is metal, to overcome wood chi moving from the East. He should be placed facing East.

The guardian of the West is Mo Li Hai. He holds a four-string mandolin, which, when played, causes great balls of fire to fall from heaven, thus destroying the metal energy of the West. He should be placed facing West.

The guardian of the South is Mo Li Hung, who carries a magic umbrella. When open, it creates total darkness, putting out the fire energy of the South. It can also unleash tidal waves and earthquakes that can destroy all negative forces. He should face South.

The guardian of the North is Mo Li Shou. He carries a pearl in one hand and a serpent in the other. Sometimes, he is shown seated on an elephant. He should face North in order to overcome the bad energy coming from there.

Shown here are (from left): Mo Li Ching, guardian of the East; Mo Li Hai, who protects the West; Mo Li Hung guardian of the South; and Mo Li Shou, guardian of the North.

Display the eight precious treasures in your home 165

The eight precious treasures symbolize prosperity, wealth, and abundance, which are manifested in eight different ways. The presence of all eight precious treasures creates a powerful spiritual ambience when you mentally offer these treasures and dedicate the good luck they bring to the highest good.

These precious treasures feature prominently in the Mandala offerings which Buddhists create in their minds as part of their daily meditation practice. These are, therefore, very powerful and important symbols, whose presence in the home adds tremendously to the creation of a calm spiritual presence within it.

These precious treasures are:

1 The precious vase, which signifies peace and serenity in a household. It is also the wealth vase, which symbolically refers to a family's wealth and assets. When you protect the vase and treat it with care, you are safeguarding your assets and also watching them multiply.

2 The precious wheel, which signifies the attainment of knowledge and the achievement of the highest scholastic honors.

3 The precious jewel, which signifies wealth in its most beautiful forms as treasures of the earth: gold, diamonds, and precious stones.

4 The precious queen, who signifies the powerful matriarchal force that keeps a family together, united, strong, and resilient.

5 The precious general, who signifies good security and protection for the home and its residents.

6 The precious minister, who takes care of all administrative matters and ensures that life flows smoothly and well.

7 The precious horse, which brings recognition and fame to the household and ensures the spread of your good name.

8 The precious elephant, which brings an abundance of male heirs into a house—a true personification of descendants' luck.

166 Magnifying sacred energy with holy objects

If you want your living space to be sacred, then having holy objects inside your home is certain to help you achieve this quickly and efficiently. Holy objects work as powerful symbols that communicate with us at higher dimensions of consciousness. These may be religious paintings and images or statues of deities. Each of the major religious traditions has truly stunning images, paintings, and works of art that can be exhibited in the home, given a respectable and prominent display space, and, if we so wish, even consecrated.

When you invite religious objects of any faith into your home, you are creating spiritual energy within it. Holy objects magnify spiritual chi just by being there. This is why so many Chinese have the image of Kuan Yin–the Goddess of Mercy/Compassion–in

If you purchase sacred art, always find out about its history and the way it should be displayed.

their homes. To many Chinese, Kuan Yin is the ultimate sacred object. They feel that her mere presence in a home imbues it with her blessings.

Treating holy objects with respect

Spiritual energy is something truly hard to explain. It must be felt and experienced. I always advise people I know that they should be very discerning when inviting holy objects into their homes. Precisely because they are sacred images, it is best to bring in only those that have a meaning for you. Do not bring in strange-looking images with which you are totally unfamiliar–you must be able to recognize images of gods and deities you display. If they come from a country you are unfamiliar with, it is always a good idea to ask how they should be exhibited and whether there may be any taboos associated with showing them.

I almost always feel a jolt when I see Buddha heads in people's homes. Although I am sure no disrespect is meant by people who display Buddha heads in their homes, nevertheless I feel a great sadness when I realize that these antique sacred objects may have been plundered from holy grounds and temples. I have also seen Kuan Yin images as lamp stands and table stands; I cringe at this disrespectful display of what to many millions of people are devotional statues. The general rule is to treat all sacred objects with the utmost respect. If you invite them into your home, place at least one offering in front of them, even if it is just a light that shines on their beauty. This way, you do not think of them as decorations, but rather as adding to the spiritual chi of the home.

Exhibiting spiritual friends from other realms   167

Some of you reading this may already be aware that we all have spiritual friends, spirit guides, and astral companions from other realms. When we cleanse our space and invite in spiritual chi, we are also opening doorways into other realms and dimensions of existence.

Those among us who are fortunate enough to have been shown a window into this invisible world know that this awareness is something that can be developed, expanded, and speeded up. So many people are now coming forward with accounts of their experiences of other realms of existence, where they speak with beings, birds, and animals, that I am now convinced we have many friends from other dimensions–many more than we know!

Coincidences and messages

In order to open the window into those worlds a little wider, you may want to consciously tune in to clues and coincidences when they happen. Become sensitive to messages from the cosmic realms. For instance, if you keep seeing a certain plant, or coming into contact with a certain animal, you may construe this as a message cutting across realms. Messages come in the books that make their way to you (even this book), in the images that come on the moment you turn on the television, the first thing you see on the road when going to work, the object of a conversation over the phone, on the bus, at work. It is the recurring themes to which you should pay attention. String these coincidences together and see whether a message is, indeed, coming to you.

Finding Spiritual Friends

Many people have affinities with certain animals, particular flowers, or a type of bird or fish. These could be your friends from another realm. The next time you attend an art show, see if anything grabs you. Note whether anything is irresistible to you. Images that tug and pull at your heart-strings always mean something.

When I first set eyes on a colorful Tibetan thangka painting, I literally drooled; I could not take my eyes off its striking images. Later, when I visited Nepal, I made my way to a thangka shop and spent two magical days going crazy over these paintings. Today my home is filled with many beautiful thangka paintings of different buddhas. Of course I love to think of these buddhas as my friends, reaching out for me through time and space and continuing to teach me as I live out this existence. Whatever they are or may be, following my instincts on this has led to a quantum leap in my spiritual consciousness.

168 Channel universal light into your home

I have come to realize that we all draw strength, courage, hope, and knowledge from a universal light source. If we did not worry about the words we use and what we mean, and instead focused on our actual experiences, then we would be halfway to accessing this universal light source.

If you create a visual image of this universal light source in your mind, and you create a channel through which light from this source flows into your home, the spiritual essence of the energy that comes into your house will fill you with a mysterious bliss. Feel this light dissolving all that is dirty, smelly, and unsavory, leaving behind only all that is beautiful, nurturing, and embracing. This process, which starts as a simple physical dejunking of

physical space and carries on to the dejunking of what is inside our minds, will surely lead us to spiritual realms and to the true cleansing of space and mind.

When you throw away the things that are holding you back, doorways open into magical realms where all things are possible and where experiences have permanently happy endings. Getting to this stage of realization requires effort, a letting go, and making a quantum leap into what is boundless. Start, then, with your own living space, and then your mind. Remember that experiences differ from person to person, and from moment to moment, but we are surely better people for having found a new, deeper level of awareness.

A clutter-free space nurtures the mind, body, and spirit, creating a special ambience in the home.

Index

Picture credits